Awakening to Reality

By the same author:

Great Clarity: Daoism and Alchemy in Early Medieval China (Stanford University Press, 2006)
The Encyclopedia of Taoism, editor (Routledge, 2008)

Awakening to Reality

The "Regulated Verses"
of the *Wuzhen pian*,
a Taoist Classic
of Internal Alchemy

Translated,
with Introduction and Notes,
by
Fabrizio Pregadio

Golden Elixir Press
2009

Golden Elixir Press
Mountain View, CA
www.goldenelixir.com

© 2009 Fabrizio Pregadio

ISBN 978-0-9843082-1-7 (pbk)

Library of Congress Control Number: 2009912822

Contents

Preface

This book has had a long gestation. I began to read *Awakening to Reality* in 1991-92, when I was a post-graduate student in Japan. Later, around 1995, I drafted a first translation of the "Regulated Verses." I went back to the text several times, and improved my translation especially in connection with courses I taught at the Technische Universität Berlin in 2000-01 and at Stanford University in 2007-08. The present version is the fruit of a thorough revision of the translation and a complete rewriting of many notes.

In its present form, the book is especially addressed to those who do not read Chinese. I have not meant to simplify what is by its own nature complex, but have tried to render the text as faithfully and to explain it as clearly as was possible for me, omitting nonessential technical details.

I am grateful to Noreen Khawaja whose comments and suggestions improved the manuscript.

Fabrizio Pregadio
November 2009

Introduction

Awakening to Reality (*Wuzhen pian*) is one of the most important and best-known Taoist alchemical texts. Written in the eleventh century, it describes in a poetical form, and in a typically cryptic and allusive language, several facets of Neidan, or internal alchemy. The present book presents the first part of the text, consisting of sixteen poems, which contain a concise but comprehensive exposition of Neidan. In addition to notes that intend to clarify the meaning of the more obscure points, the book also contains selections from a commentary dating from the late eighteenth century, which is distinguished by the use of a lucid and plain language.

ZHANG BODUAN AND HIS WORK

The author of *Awakening to Reality* is Zhang Boduan, also known as True Man of Purple Yang (Ziyang zhenren). As is common with many Taoist adepts, his biography combines fact and legend, and the dates of the main events in his life are not entirely certain. He was born in Tiantai, a district in the present-day southeastern province of Zhejiang, probably in 987. Having concluded his education with the highest degree, he undertook a career as an administrative officer in his district. Soon, however, he was accused of committing a major infraction in his duties and was punished with banishment to the remote south, in the Guangdong province. Around 1065 he moved to Sichuan, in the southwestern part of China, with an army commander that had hired him as advisor. While he was in Sichuan he met a master who transmitted alchemical teachings to him, and a few years later he wrote his work. Later he moved to the southern Yunnan province, where, having made sure that his work would survive him, he died in 1082.[1]

---

[1] This account of Zhang Boduan's life is based on Baldrian-Hussein, "Zhang Boduan."

In addition to *Awakening to Reality*, three other alchemical texts are attributed to Zhang Boduan:

1   *Wuzhen pian shiyi* (Supplement to *Awakening to Reality*)
2   *Yuqing jinsi Qinghua biwen jinbao neilian danjue* (Alchemical Instructions on the Inner Refinement of the Golden Treasure, a Secret Text from the Golden Casket of the Jade Clarity Transmitted by the Immortal of Green Florescence)
3   *Jindan sibai zi* (Four Hundred Words on the Golden Elixir)

Although doubts have been cast on Zhang Boduan's authorship of these works, at least one of them, the *Jindan sibai zi*, bears a visible affinity to *Awakening to Reality* in content and language.[2]

The *Awakening* is divided into three main parts, all of which consist of poems written in different meters. The first part, which is translated here, contains sixteen poems written in "regulated verses" (eight-line heptasyllabic poems, known as *lüshi*). The second part contains sixty-four poems written in "cut-off lines" (four-line heptasyllabic poems, *jueju*). The third part contains eighteen poems, written in different meters and divided into three sets: one pentasyllabic poem, twelve "lyrics" (*ci*) of irregular length, and five more poems in "cut-off lines." The number of poems in each part of the work has a symbolic value. The sixteen poems in the first part represent the principle of the "two eights," which refers to the state of balance of the Yin and Yang components of the Elixir (see the note to Poem 7, lines 7-8). The sixty-four poems in the second part represent the hexagrams of the *Book of Changes* (*Yijing*; they are not, however, concerned with the hexagrams themselves). In the third part, the single pentasyllabic poem represents the original state of Unity; the twelve lyrics represent the twelve stages of the "fire times" (the heating of the Elixir; see Poem 5, lines 5-6); and the final five poems represent the five agents (*wuxing*).

Since the time of its creation, *Awakening to Reality* has enjoyed a wide circulation that has continued to the present day. In the thirteenth century, Zhang Boduan was placed at the origin of Nanzong, the Southern Lineage of Neidan, and his work became the main textual source of that lineage. Nanzong consists of a series of five masters whose works describe forms of Neidan closely related to one another (in addition to

---

[2] The *Jindan sibai zi* has been translated by Davis and Chao, "Four Hundred Word Chin Tan of Chang Po-tuan," and by Cleary, *The Inner Teachings of Taoism*, 1-32.

displaying similar formal features, such as the use of poetry). After Zhang Boduan, the lineage continues with Shi Tai (?-1158), the author of the *Huanyuan pian* (Reverting to the Source); Xue Daoguang (1078?-1191), the author of the *Huandan fuming pian* (Returning to Life through the Reverted Elixir); Chen Nan (?-1213), the author of the *Cuixu pian* (The Emerald Emptiness); and finally Bai Yuchan (1194-1229?), to whom is ascribed authorship of a large number of works and who is also known as a specialist of the Taoist Thunder Rites (*leifa*).[3]

While transmission among the latter four masters is historical, Shi Tai was not Zhang Boduan's direct disciple. It is now understood that the Southern Lineage had, in its beginnings, no conventionally recognized form or structure, and was formally established as a lineage only at a later time, possibly by Bai Yuchan himself. The nomination of its five masters as the Five Patriarchs (*wuzu*) was inspired by the identical designation used within the Northern Lineage (Beizong), better known as Quanzhen or Complete Reality. Later, Li Daochun (fl. 1288-92) and Chen Zhixu (1290-after 1335), both of whom are among the greatest representatives of the Neidan tradition, took up the task of integrating Nanzong within Quanzhen. By their time, it was held that the anonymous master who gave alchemical teachings to Zhang Boduan in Sichuan was no other than Liu Haichan, the fourth (or fifth, according to different lists) patriarch of Quanzhen. Liu Haichan, in turn, was said to have received those teachings from Zhongli Quan and Lü Dongbin, both of whom were also included among the Quanzhen patriarchs. As a result of this conflation, Nanzong ceased to exist as an independent lineage and became part of Quanzhen. Its five masters and their texts, nevertheless, are still seen as representing one of the most important forms of Taoist internal alchemy.

DOCTRINES

Internal alchemy is not a "school" of Taoism, but rather one of its major traditions, and as such it has existed in forms that differ, sometimes considerably, from one another. Certain forms of internal alchemy give priority to its purely spiritual aspect, while others emphasize the performance of practices. Like all traditional doctrines, moreover, internal alchemy defies attempts of systematization. For these reasons, a full

---

[3] On these authors and their works see Boltz, *A Survey of Taoist Literature*, 173-79, and the relevant entries in Pregadio, ed., *The Encyclopedia of Taoism*.

description of Taoist internal alchemy is beyond the scope of this introduction. The following pages intend only to provide a few basic tools that
should make the understanding of *Awakening to Reality* easier.[4]

Doctrinal sources

Texts of internal alchemy contain repeated references or allusions—for
example, by the use of certain distinctive terms—to the major sources of
Taoist thought, namely the *Daode jing* (Book of the Way and its Virtue)
and the *Zhuangzi* (Book of Master Zhuang). In particular, the *Daode jing*—
which virtually all Taoists in China have considered to be the fountain-
head of the entire Taoist tradition—has provided alchemy with essential
doctrinal foundations: the view of the Dao (the Way), the notion that the
generation of the world by the Dao is best described as a sequence of
stages, and the basic principle of "returning to the Dao" (*fandao*). The
above-mentioned Chen Zhixu says in his major work, the *Jindan dayao*
(Great Essentials of the Golden Elixir, chapter 2): "The Way of Laozi is the
great Way of the Golden Elixir."[5]

In the "Regulated Verses" of his *Awakening to Reality*, Zhang Boduan
refers several times to the *Daode jing* (see especially Poem 4, lines 1-2;
Poem 6, line 3; and Poem 12, line 5). The same is true of the *Zhuangzi*, a
work that has provided countless Taoist authors with both poetical
inspiration and technical terms (examples of both are found in Poem 5,
line 2, and Poem 6, lines 5-6). Even though these references might appear
to be occasional, or even superficial, they reflect a distinctive aspect of
Chinese literature, especially philosophical or religious: it is often by
means of short and apparently casual allusions that authors signal their
bonds to specific doctrines or teachings.

Zhang Boduan is said to have devoted himself to Chan (Zen) Buddhism late in life, and one of the works that are ascribed to him, the
Wuzhen pian shiyi (Supplement to *Awakening to Reality*), has a strong

---

[4] The scholarly work that reflects the deepest understanding of Neidan is
Robinet, *Introduction à l'alchimie intérieure taoïste*. Shorter accounts are available in
Robinet, "Original Contributions of Neidan to Taoism and Chinese Thought," and
in Pregadio and Skar, "Inner Alchemy (Neidan)."

[5] It should be clear that what Chen Zhixu calls the Way of Laozi does not
necessarily need the Way of the Golden Elixir, which—generally speaking—is one
of several ways that make it possible to approach the doctrines of the *Daode jing*.
On the contrary, instead, the Way of the Golden Elixir does need the Way of Laozi,
which provides alchemy with its indispensable doctrinal basis.

Buddhist background. Like many other Neidan texts, the *Awakening* also contains Buddhist expressions, for example in the first poem.[6] Connections between Taoism and Buddhism are, in fact, indicated in a most explicit way by the title of Zhang Boduan's work, which combines a typically Buddhist term, *wu* or "awakening," with a typically Taoist term, *zhen* or "reality, truth, perfection." (The term *wu* is better known in the West in its Japanese pronunciation, *satori*, which denotes the "awakening" in the Chan/Zen Buddhist tradition.)[7] These connections are perhaps best explained by the fact that Neidan is ultimately a way of seeing, and therefore recognizes the validity of any formulation of doctrinal points that are analogous to its own doctrines, often crossing the border between established traditions. Buddhism is one of the traditions—in fact, the most important one—from which Neidan has acquired concepts and vocabulary.

The same is fundamentally true of Confucian ideas, even though the "Regulated Verses" do not contain examples of their use; in fact, an allusion to Confucianism found at the beginning of the text (Poem 1, line 2) is distinctly negative. This allusion, however, concerns the definition of the highest ideal for the human being, a subject on which Confucianism and Taoism definitely differ. In other contexts, alchemical texts do contain Confucian terminology and even short quotations from Confucian texts for reasons analogous to those mentioned above with regard to Buddhism. Examples will be found in the translations of passages from Liu Yiming's commentary, where the author freely uses Confucian vocabulary (for example, "innate knowledge," or *liangzhi*, and "innate capacity, or *liangneng*).

As far as alchemical texts are concerned, Zhang Boduan's main source is, beyond any doubt, the *Zhouyi cantong qi* (Token for Joining the Three, in Accordance with the *Book of Changes*). This work, traditionally dated to the second century CE, but in fact written—or at least completed—a few centuries later, has supplied the entire Neidan tradition with doctrines, imagery, and terminology, and with the basic models of its practices. *Awakening to Reality* has even been called a commentary on the *Cantong qi*. This definition is probably an overstatement, but it is a fact

---

[6] In addition to stating that "The Way of Laozi is the great Way of the Golden Elixir," the above-mentioned Chen Zhixu also writes in his *Jindan dayao* (chapter 14): "The Way of Bodhidharma is the Way of the Golden Elixir." Bodhidharma is traditionally considered to be the originator of Chan Buddhism.

[7] The third word in the Chinese title of the *Awakening, pian*, generically designates a "piece of writing."

that the "Regulated Verses" contain many allusions to the *Cantong qi*, and that at least one passage of the text (Poem 5, lines 5-6) would be hardly comprehensible without reading a parallel passage in the *Cantong qi*.[8]

The Elixir

Precelestial and postcelestial domains. At the basis of alchemy, and of other spiritual teachings, is the perception that the world exists in two fundamental states, the unconditioned and the conditioned ones. Whether this distinction "truly" exists is a question that internal alchemy approaches at an advanced stage (in particular, as we shall see, at the very last stage of its practice); the initial awareness of this distinction constitutes, nevertheless, the beginning of its path.

Using two traditional Chinese terms, the unconditioned and conditioned domains are respectively defined as precelestial (or prior to Heaven, *xiantian*, lit. "before Heaven") and postcelestial (or posterior to Heaven, *houtian*, lit. "after Heaven").[9] The postcelestial domain is distinguished by multiplicity and relativity; it is the state that features transitory events and phenomena that succeed one another within space and time. The precelestial domain, in one of the approximations that might be used to describe it, is the constant and omnipresent original state of Oneness, which contains all events and phenomena independently of whether they do or do not occur, and with no distinctions of space and time, here and there, before and after.

In this view, the cosmos as we know it is the self-manifestation of the Dao, which first determines itself as Oneness. Primal Oneness contains Yin and Yang in their pristine state; the joining of Yin and Yang generates the world. To appreciate the details of this view, it is convenient to follow the example of the alchemical texts and describe it through the emblems of the *Book of Changes*. Qian ☰ (pristine Yang) and Kun ☷ (pristine Yin) are constantly joined to one another in the state of Unity. Being joined,

---

[8] The best English translation of the *Cantong qi* is found in Bertschinger, *The Secret of Everlasting Life*. Unfortunately, however, this book does not offer the tools that are necessary to comprehend the extremely difficult imagery and terminology of the text.

[9] *Xiantian* and *houtian* are often translated as "former Heaven" and "later Heaven." Both terms are related to the phrase *xian tiandi sheng* ("born before Heaven and Earth") found in the *Daode jing*, the *Zhuangzi*, and other early texts. The *Daode jing*, for example, says (chapter 25): "There is something inchoate and yet accomplished, born before Heaven and Earth. . . . I do not know its name, but call it Dao."

Qian unceasingly bestows its essence to Kun, and Kun brings it to achievement; thus the world with its countless events and phenomena is generated. However, due to the very fact of being continuously joined to one another, Qian becomes Li ☲ (Yang), and Kun becomes Kan ☵ (Yin). Therefore the essence of the Yang principle in its pure state is now found within Kan. That principle, which is the One Breath of the Dao (the state of Unity represented by the undivided line), is what an alchemist seeks to recover.

Table 1. Schematic representation of the precelestial and postcelestial states, with cosmological and alchemical terms and emblems used to describe them.

"Inversion" and the generation of the Elixir. Alchemy offers a way to return to the state of Unity. In its view, the forward movement (*shun*, lit. "continuation") from the Dao to the ten thousand things can be compensated by a reverse, backward movement (*ni*, "inversion"). The inversion process is represented in internal alchemy in several different ways, each of which uses different images and terms. The most common formulation refers to Essence (*jing*), Breath (*qi*), and Spirit (*shen*). The Dao, which first self-manifests as pure Spirit, issues its Breath, which in turn coalesces into

Essence, the seed that gives birth to the world.[10] Human beings are composed with the same three elements. Accordingly, in its most typical codification, the alchemical process is based on the progressive refining of those components. The refining occurs in an inverted sequence, which reintegrates each component into the previous one:

(1) Refining Essence into Breath (*lianjing huaqi*)
(2) Refining Breath into Spirit (*lianqi huashen*)
(3) Refining Spirit and reverting to Emptiness (*lianshen huanxu*)

The Elixir itself is also described with different terminology: it may be called the One Breath of the Dao, Pure Yang, Gold, Lead, and with literally dozens of other appellations.[11] Liu Yiming (1734-1821), in a passage of his commentary to *Awakening to Reality* translated in the present book, writes that "there is no other Golden Elixir outside one's fundamental nature," and that "every human being has this Golden Elixir complete in himself." In his view, the Elixir is the essential, unchanging true nature of the human being; it has, fundamentally, no form and no name. However, one of the most widespread and best-known images used to represent the Elixir, also adopted by *Awakening to Reality*, is that of an embryo, an infant, or a child. When the Elixir is depicted in this way, the three stages mentioned above respectively correspond to the conception, the gestation, and the birth of an immortal infant. Its conception occurs in the lower Cinnabar Field (*dantian*), located in the region of the abdomen; its gestation, in the middle Cinnabar Field, in the region of the heart; and its birth, in the upper Cinnabar Field, in the region of the brain. At the end of the process, the child is described as exiting the individual from the top of his head. Neidan texts refer to this event as the

---

[10] The word *jing*, which here denotes Essence, also denotes the male sexual semen. This essence is the seed that Qian, the masculine, creative aspect of the Dao, entrusts to Kun, its feminine, accomplishing aspect. Since Qian and Kun are the primary modes that the Dao takes on its self-manifestation, it might be said that the Dao is both the "father" and the "mother" of the world.

[11] The denomination of the Elixir as Lead may at first be confusing, but the rationale should be clear by looking at table 1 above. Lead has three values in alchemy: (1) black or native lead, which is the Yin principle in the conditioned state; (2) True Lead, which is the True Yang principle now found within Yin; (3) the One Breath of the Dao, which is described as Pure Yang, the state prior to the subdivision of the One into the Two. All three values of Lead are represented by the undivided line of the *Book of Changes*.

birth of a *shen wai zhi shen*, an expression that can be understood as "a body outside one's body," or as "a self outside one's self."

Cosmological emblems

Once the world is generated, it is subject to the laws of the cosmic domain. Neidan texts constantly bring this domain to the fore, and explain its features by means of the standard Chinese cosmological system. It would be virtually impossible to understand the language and imagery of *Awakening to Reality*, and of internal alchemy in general, without acquiring a basic familiarity with this system.[12]

At the basis of Chinese cosmology are several sets of emblems, all related to one another. The most important sets are the five agents, the ten celestial stems, the twelve earthly branches, and the eight trigrams and sixty-four hexagrams of the *Book of Changes* (*Yijing*). Each set represents a different way of understanding and explicating the main features of the cosmos. However, despite the variety of emblems, the fundamental underlying notion in internal alchemy, and in Taoism as a whole, is that those emblems make it possible to describe the subdivision of the One into the many, and the reverse process that makes it possible to return from multiplicity to Unity. For example, the five agents are used to represent how the original One Breath issued from the Dao takes on five main different modes in the cosmos; but the central agent, Soil, represents the One Breath itself, and the process that occurs in internal alchemy has been be described as the reduction of the agents to one, namely, Soil.[13]

The individual items in any set of emblems—for example, the individual agents in the set of the five agents—can be thought of as "categories" to which all phenomena and events in the cosmos can be assigned. The emblems themselves are entirely abstract; they gain meaning only in relation to one another, and in connection with the

[12] The Chinese cosmological system, which was fully developed as early as the third or the second century BCE, is not specifically Taoist. It evolved with contributions from specialists of various traditional sciences, including diviners, astronomers, and physicians, and from thinkers belonging to different currents. Taoism is only one of several traditions that have contributed to, and drawn upon, this system.

[13] See, for example, the *Cantong qi* (chapter 11 in Chen Zhixu's redaction): "When Water flourishes, Fire is extinguished, and both die, together returning to generous Soil. Now, the three natures have joined together, for their fundamental natures share an ancestor in common."

9

types of entities and phenomena that they represent. This implies that the author of a text can mention any of these emblems, and immediately bring up all of the associated entities. A mention of the agent Wood, for example, evokes the east, the spring, the liver, the Yang principle in its emerging state, and True Yin within Yang. It is the reader's task to understand which of those entities—for example, a segment of a temporal cycle, or an organ of the human body—is relevant, or most relevant, in a particular context. This feature constitutes, on its own, one of the main difficulties in reading and understanding Chinese alchemical texts.

Five agents. As said above, the five agents (*wuxing*; see tables 2 and 3) are five emblematic modes taken on by Original Breath (*yuanqi*) in the cosmos. These modes are represented by Wood, Fire, Soil, Metal, and Water.

In internal alchemy, Wood represents True Yin, and Metal represents True Yang. Accordingly, the ingredients of the Elixir are often referred to Wood and Metal. The same, however, is true of Water and Fire, respectively. In addition, internal alchemy assigns a crucial role to Soil. Being placed at the center, Soil stands for the source from which the other four agents derive, and therefore guarantees the conjunction of the world of multiplicity to the original state of Unity. One of the typical representations of the alchemical process (also mentioned in *Awakening to Reality*, see Poem 14) is the reduction of the five agents to three and then to one. The whole process happens by the virtue of Soil, which acts as "mediator" between True Yin and True Yang and makes their conjunction possible (see the note to Poem 3, line 5).

Stems and branches. The ten celestial stems (*tiangan*) and the twelve earthly branches (*dizhi*) are two sets of emblems used to refer to a variety of items (see tables 4 and 5). The stems are primarily related, in pairs, to the five agents and, through them, to all sets of entities associated with the five agents. The branches are used to represent the months of the year, the "double hours" of the day, and other sets consisting of twelve items.[14]

---

[14] The Chinese divided the day into twelve parts, usually referred to as "double hours" in English. The twelve earthly branches are not used in the "Regulated Verses." They are mentioned in this introduction because of their close association with the ten stems.

10

	WOOD	FIRE	SOIL	METAL	WATER
DIRECTIONS	east	south	center	west	north
SEASONS	spring	summer	(midsummer)	autumn	winter
COLORS	green (or blue)	red	yellow	white	black
EMBLEMATIC ANIMALS	green dragon	vermilion bird	yellow dragon	white tiger	snake and turtle
NUMBERS	3, 8	2, 7	5, 10	4, 9	1, 6
YIN-YANG (1)	minor Yang	great Yang	balance	minor Yin	great Yin
YIN-YANG (2)	True Yin	Yang	balance	True Yang	Yin
NOTES	*jiao* 角	*zhi* 徵	*gong* 宮	*shang* 商	*yu* 羽
STEMS	*jia* 甲 *yi* 乙	*bing* 丙 *ding* 丁	*wu* 戊 *ji* 己	*geng* 庚 *xin* 辛	*ren* 壬 *gui* 癸
BRANCHES	*yin* 寅 *mao* 卯	*wu* 午 *si* 巳	*xu* 戌, *chou* 丑 *wei* 未, *chen* 辰	*you* 酉 *shen* 申	*hai* 亥 *zi* 子
PLANETS	Jupiter	Mars	Saturn	Venus	Mercury
VISCERA	liver	heart	spleen	lungs	kidneys
RECEPTACLES	gall-bladder	small intestine	stomach	large intestine	urinary bladder
BODY ORGAN	eyes	tongue	mouth	nose	ears
EMOTIONS	anger	joy	ratiocination	sorrow	apprehension
TASTES	sour	bitter	sweet	acrid	salty
CLIMATES	wind	hot	moist	dry	cold
RELATIONS	father	daughter	ancestors	mother	son

Table 2. The five agents (*wuxing*) and their associations.

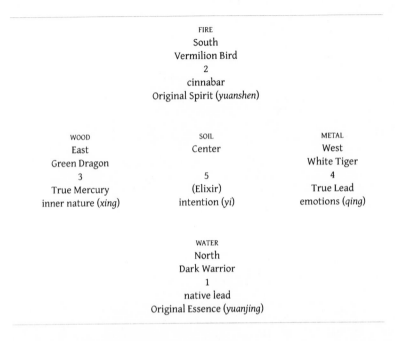

FIRE
South
Vermilion Bird
2
cinnabar
Original Spirit (*yuanshen*)

WOOD	SOIL	METAL
East	Center	West
Green Dragon		White Tiger
3	5	4
True Mercury	(Elixir)	True Lead
inner nature (*xing*)	intention (*yi*)	emotions (*qing*)

WATER
North
Dark Warrior
1
native lead
Original Essence (*yuanjing*)

Table 3. Spatial arrangement of the five agents (*wuxing*), with some of the main associations relevant to internal alchemy. In agreement with traditional Chinese conventions, North is shown at the bottom, South at the top, East on the left, and West on the right.

In the "Regulated Verses" of *Awakening to Reality*, four of the ten celestial stems are especially important. *Wu* and *ji* (nos. 5 and 6) are related to the agent Soil. Taken together they represent, therefore, the One, the original state of unity of the five agents that the alchemical process intends to restore. More exactly, *wu* and *ji* represent the Yang and Yin halves of the One, respectively, and it is by means of them that Soil can act as a mediator in joining Yin and Yang (see Poem 3, line 5). Two other stems, *ren* and *gui* (nos. 9 and 10), respectively represent the precelestial and the postcelestial aspects of Water, which gives birth to True Lead, or True Yang (see Poem 7, line 3, and Poem 11, line 4).

	STEMS		AGENTS	DIRECTIONS	COLORS	VISCERA	NUMBERS
1	jia	甲	WOOD	east	green	liver	3, 8
2	yi	乙					
3	bing	丙	FIRE	south	red	heart	2, 7
4	ding	丁					
5	wu	戊	SOIL	center	yellow	spleen	5
6	ji	己					
7	geng	庚	METAL	west	white	lungs	4, 9
8	xin	辛					
9	ren	壬	WATER	north	black	kidneys	1, 6
10	gui	癸					

Table 4. The ten celestial stems (*tiangan*) and their associations.

	BRANCHES		AGENTS	DIRECTIONS	HOURS	ANIMALS	NUMBERS
1	zi	子	WATER	N	23–1	rat	1, 6
2	chou	丑	SOIL	NNE 3/4 E	1–3	ox	5, 10
3	yin	寅	WOOD	ENE 3/4 N	3–5	tiger	3, 8
4	mao	卯	WOOD	E	5–7	rabbit	3, 8
5	chen	辰	SOIL	ESE 3/4 S	7–9	dragon	5, 10
6	si	巳	FIRE	SSE 3/4 E	9–11	snake	2, 7
7	wu	午	FIRE	S	11–13	horse	2, 7
8	wei	未	SOIL	SSW 3/4 W	13–15	sheep	5, 10
9	shen	申	METAL	WSW 3/4 S	15–17	monkey	4, 9
10	you	酉	METAL	W	17–19	rooster	4, 9
11	xu	戌	SOIL	WNW 3/4 N	19–21	dog	5, 10
12	hai	亥	WATER	NNW 3/4 W	21–23	pig	1, 6

Table 5. The twelve earthly branches (*dizhi*) and their associations.

Trigrams and hexagrams. The last major set of cosmological emblems used in *Awakening to Reality* consists of the trigrams and hexagrams of the *Book of Changes* (*Yijing*). Alchemical texts, and Taoist texts in general, are not interested in the *Book of Changes* as a divination manual. Instead, they use its trigrams and hexagrams as cosmological emblems.[15]

The eight trigrams are made of different combinations of three lines, which can be either Yin -- (broken) or Yang — (solid). In a most basic way, the trigrams are associated with natural phenomena and with relations among family members (see table 6). In Taoism and in alchemy, however, the trigrams are used as abstract emblems, analogous and related to the other sets of emblems mentioned before. To give one example, the eight trigrams are used to refer to the directions of space: four of them represent the cardinal directions (just like four of the five agents), and the other four represent the intermediate directions.

☰	☱	☲	☳	☴	☵	☶	☷
乾	兌	離	震	巽	坎	艮	坤
QIAN	DUI	LI	ZHEN	XUN	KAN	GEN	KUN
heaven	lake	fire	thunder	wind	water	mountain	earth
father	youngest daughter	second daughter	eldest son	eldest daughter	second son	youngest son	mother
south	southeast	east	northeast	southwest	west	northwest	north
northwest	west	south	east	southeast	north	northeast	southwest

Table 6. The eight trigrams and their main associations: elements in nature, family relations, and directions in the cosmological configurations "prior to Heaven" (*xiantian*) and "posterior to Heaven" (*houtian*).

[15] The main textual basis for this use of trigrams and hexagrams is one of the appendixes to the *Book of Changes*, entitled "Appended Sayings" ("Xici"). This appendix is translated by Wilhelm, *I Ching or Book of Changes*, 280-355, as "The Great Treatise."

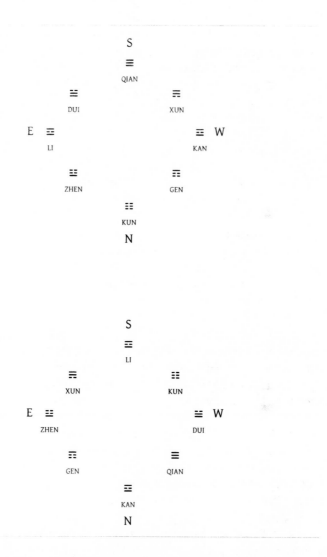

Table 7. Arrangement of the eight trigrams in the cosmological configurations "prior to Heaven" (*xiantian*, top) and "posterior to Heaven" (*houtian*, bottom).

When the eight trigrams are joined to one another in pairs, they form the sixty-four hexagrams, which are emblems made of six lines. The hexagrams represent primary states and circumstances that occur in the cosmos, in human society, or in individual existence, such as "peace," "conflict," "return," "obstruction," "following," etc.

The trigrams and hexagrams of the *Book of Changes* are used in alchemy in three main ways. First, and most frequently, four of the eight trigrams are chosen to represent the main states of Yin and Yang:

Qian	☰	True Yang in its pure state
Kun	☷	True Yin in its pure state
Kan	☵	Yin containing True Yang
Li	☲	Yang containing True Yin

In the postcelestial state, as we have seen, True Yin and True Yang are found within entities of the opposite sign. When it is represented by these emblems, the alchemical process consists in exchanging the inner lines of Kan and Li: as soon as those lines are exchanged, Qian and Kun are restored, and as soon as Qian and Kun are restored, the Elixir is generated.[16]

Second, the eight trigrams have been traditionally arranged in two main ways, known as the precelestial (*xiantian*) and the postcelestial (*houtian*) arrangements (see table 7). The precelestial arrangement represents the original state of the cosmos; the postcelestial one, its present state, the world in which we live. In the postcelestial arrangement, the positions originally occupied by Qian ☰ and Kun ☷ have been taken by Kan ☵ and Li ☲, which, once again, harbor and hide True Yin and True Yang. Qian and Kun, instead, have been displaced to the northwest and the southwest, respectively. Since the inner line of Kan ☵ is the True Yang sought by the alchemist, and this line is born within Kun ☷ when it joins with Qian ☰, Poem 7 of the *Awakening* says that "the place where the Medicine is born is just at the southwest."

Third, twelve of the sixty-four hexagrams are chosen to represent a complete cycle of ascent and descent of Yin and Yang within the main cosmic temporal cycles. These twelve hexagrams are known in Chinese cosmology as the "sovereign hexagrams" (*bigua*; see table 8). The first six hexagrams depict the rise of the Yang principle in the first half of the

---

[16] This "process" can happen in one instant, as Liu Yiming says in a passage of his commentary to the *Awakening* translated in the present book. It is, instead, gradual in the alchemical practice.

year, or of the day; the last six hexagrams depict the decline of the Yang principle, and the concurrent rise of the Yin principle, in the second half of the year, or of the day.

䷗	䷒	䷊	䷡	䷪	䷀	䷫	䷠	䷋	䷓	䷖	䷁
復	臨	泰	大壯	夬	乾	姤	遯	否	觀	剝	坤
FU	LIN	TAI	DAZHUANG	GUAI	QIAN	GOU	DUN	PI	GUAN	BO	KUN

Table 8. The twelve "sovereign hexagrams" (*bigua*).

The cycle of the twelve "sovereign hexagrams" has served as a model for the so-called "fire times" (*huohou*) in the practices of both external and internal alchemy. Fire is progressively increased in the first half of the cycle, then progressively decreased in the second half of the cycle. The whole cycle is repeated until the Elixir coalesces in the tripod (external alchemy) or in the lower Cinnabar Field (internal alchemy).

Final remarks

In a strict sense, as we have seen, alchemy consists in the recovery of the One Breath prior to Heaven, symbolized by True Lead. The adept rises through the different states of Being until he reaches the highest point, Non-Being or Emptiness; this is typically done by means of the alchemical practice, in the ways briefly outlined above.

Certain authors of texts of internal alchemy emphasize that this is only the first part of a longer process, and that the alchemical path is fulfilled only when the second part is also performed. Although they are not eager to provide too many details on this subject, they say that the alchemical practice pertains to "doing" (*youwei*): one performs the practice with a purpose in mind, and *in order to* achieve a result. To be entirely fulfilled, the alchemical way requires another inversion: a new movement of descent from "above" to "below," from Non-Being to Being, from emptiness to existence, that realizes their non-duality. This is done as one enters the state of "non-doing" (*wuwei*).

The alchemical practice prepares one to enter that state: the final stage, "refining Spirit and reverting to Emptiness," requires non-doing to be performed (see Poem 13, lines 5-6). At that point, the way of seeing radically changes. The One Breath prior to Heaven has at last been found; not only does it not need to be sought any longer, but continuing to seek it would be harmful. For the first time, the focus shifts from Lead to Mercury: one should decrease Lead and augment Mercury, bestowing the qualities of the newly found Gold to what once appeared as corrupt matter. The world to which one returns is entirely different from the world that had been left behind. The alchemical practice has brought it back to be what it is: one with the One Breath.

NOTE ON THE TRANSLATION

This translation of the "Regulated Verses" of *Awakening to Reality* is based on the Daozang (Taoist Canon) edition of the *Ziyang zhenren Wuzhen pian sanzhu* (Three Commentaries to *Awakening to Reality* by the True Man of Purple Yang), composed by Chen Zhixu (1290-after 1335).

In addition to this work, I have consulted the following sources:

1 *Wuzhen pian* (*Awakening to Reality*), in *Xiuzhen shishu* (Ten Books for the Cultivation of Reality; late thirteenth or early fourteenth centuries), chapters 26-30. Daozang edition.

2 *Ziyang zhenren Wuzhen pian zhushu* (Commentary and Subcommentary to *Awakening to Reality* by the True Man of Purple Yang), by Weng Baoguang (preface dated 1173), edited by Dai Qizong (preface dated 1335). Daozang edition.

3 *Wuzhen pian zhushi* (Commentary and Exegesis to *Awakening to Reality*), by Weng Baoguang. Daozang edition.

4 *Wuzhen pian xiaoxu* (A Short Introduction to *Awakening to Reality*), by Lu Xixing (1520-1601 or 1606), found in his collected works, *Fanghu waishi* (The External Secretary of Mount Fanghu). Edition of 1915, repr. in *Daozang jinghua* (Essential Splendors of the Taoist Canon), vol. 2:8 (Taipei: Ziyou chubanshe, 1982).

5 *Wuzhen zhizhi* (Straightforward Directions on *Awakening to Reality*), by Liu Yiming (1734-1821), found in his collected works, *Daoshu shier zhong* (Twelve Books on the Dao). Jiangdong shuju edition of 1913, repr. Xinwenfeng chubanshe (Taipei, 1975 and 1983).

6 *Wuzhen pian jizhu* (Collected Commentaries to *Awakening to Reality*), by Qiu Zhaoao (preface dated 1703). Edition of 1703, repr. in *Qigong*

yangsheng congshu (Collectanea on Qigong and Nourishing Life; Shanghai: Guji chubanshe, 1989).

The main variants found in these additional sources are reported in the Textual Notes. With few exceptions, I do not report different grammatical particles, inversion of graphs in compound words, and other minor variants that have little or no consequence on meaning.

The annotations found in the masterful work by Wang Mu, *Wuzhen pian qianjie* (A Simple Explanation of *Awakening to Reality*; 1990), have been invaluable to understand several passages of the text. In addition to this work, I have also occasionally referred to those by Zhang Zhenguo (2001) and by Liu Guoliang and Lian Yao (2005; see the bibliography at the end of the book).

Previous translations of the *Awakening* that I have consulted include those by Tenney L. Davis and Chao Yün-ts'ung (1939),[17] Thomas Cleary (1987),[18] Isabelle Robinet (1995),[19] and Paul Crowe (2000).[20]

The selections from Liu Yiming's commentary are translated from source no. 5 above. A complete translation of this commentary is included in Thomas Cleary's translation of the *Awakening*. My translations differ, sometimes considerably, from those given by Cleary.

In translating the text of Zhang Boduan's work, I have tried to preserve the original structure of the verses, which includes a subdivision into two parts (respectively made of 4 and 3 characters) in each line, typical of the "regulated verses." For obvious reasons, reflecting this feature of Zhang Boduan's poetry in English has not always been possible. I have, nevertheless, divided each Chinese line into two parts even when I have been compelled to change the original syntactic structure.

[17] Davis and Chao Yün-ts'ung, "Chang Po-tuan of T'ien-t'ai, his *Wu Chên P'ien, Essay on the Understanding of the Truth*" (full translation, based on the *Zhushu* version of Weng Baoguang's text and on Chen Zhixu's text).

[18] Cleary, *Understanding Reality: A Taoist Alchemical Classic* (full translation, based on Liu Yiming's text).

[19] Robinet, *Introduction à l'alchimie intérieure taoïste*, 205-54 (full translation, based on Chen Zhixu's text).

[20] Crowe, "Chapters on *Awakening to the Real*" (translation of the "Regulated Verses," based on the *Xiuzhen shishu* text).

Translation

Poem 1

1   *If you do not search for the Great Dao*
and do not leave the delusive paths,
you may be endowed with worthiness and talent,
but would you be a great man?
3   *One hundred years of age*
are a spark sent forth from a stone,
a whole lifetime
is a bubble floating on the water.

5   *You only covet profit and emolument*
and search for nothing more than glory and fame,
without considering that your body
covertly withers and decays.
7   *Let me ask you — Even if you pile up gold*
as high as one of the sacred mountains,
bribing impermanence would be impossible,
wouldn't it?

其一

1   不求大道出迷途
       縱負賢材豈丈夫
3   百歲光陰石火爍
       一生身世水泡浮

5   只貪利祿求榮顯
       不顧形容暗悴枯
7   試問堆金等山嶽
       無常買得不來無

NOTES ON POEM 1

The first two poems introduce *Awakening to Reality* with reminders on the transitoriness of life. The common ways of the world, says Zhang Boduan, are ephemeral and delusive. Only by following the Dao can one rise beyond impermanence.

1   *If you do not search for the Great Dao and do not leave the delusive paths.*

Note the parallel between a Taoist expression ("search for the Great Dao") and a Buddhist expression ("leave the delusive paths"). As a Buddhist term, "delusive paths" (*mitu*) refers to the Three Realms (*sanjie*) and the six ways of conditioned existence (*liudao*, also called *liuqu* or six directions of reincarnation). The Three Realms are the realm of sensuous desire, the realm of form, and the realm of absence of form. The Six Ways of conditioned existence are the hells, the hungry ghosts, the animals, the malevolent nature spirits, the human existence, and the gods.

2   *You may be endowed with worthiness and talent, but would you be a great man?*

After a Taoist and a Buddhist expression, Zhang Boduan uses a Confucian term, "worthiness and talent" (*xiancai*), that defines the model virtues of scholars and officials. He contrasts these virtues with those of the "great man" (*zhangfu*), a classical term that denotes the person who has realized the Dao.

8   *Bribing impermanence would be impossible, wouldn't it?*

Impermanence is another Buddhist notion. However, the term *wuchang*, literally meaning "non-constant," also has a specific use in Taoism, where it denotes the transient ways (paths, pursuits) that differ from the "constant" Way, the Dao. See the opening words of the *Daode jing* (Book of the Way and its Virtue, chapter 1): "A way that can be determined as a way is not the constant Way." — Wang Mu suggests that *wuchang* in this sentence means "the end of life." According to this view, the sentence should be translated as: "Bribing death would be impossible, wouldn't it?"

Poem 2

1   *Whilst human life may have*
a span of one hundred years,
longevity or early death, exhaustion or accomplishment
cannot be known in advance.
3   *Yesterday you were on the street*
riding on horseback,
this morning in your coffin
you are already a sleeping corpse.

5   *Your wife and wealth are cast off,*
they are not in your possession;
retribution for your faults is about to come —
now you can hardly fool yourself.
7   *If you do not search for the Great Medicine,*
how can you ever come upon it?
But coming upon it and not refining it,
this is truly foolish and insane.

其二

1   人生雖有百年期
壽夭窮通莫預知
3   昨日街頭方走馬
今朝棺內已眠屍

5   妻財抛下非君有
罪業將行難自欺
7   大藥不求爭得遇
遇之不鍊是愚癡

NOTES ON POEM 2

Zhang Boduan again reminds his readers that existence is transient and ephemeral; one may follow delusive paths in life, but at the time of death deception is no longer possible. Therefore one should seek the teachings of the Golden Elixir, which make it possible to transcend this condition. But merely hearing about the Golden Elixir is not sufficient: one must also devote oneself to its cultivation.

1   *Whilst human life may have a span of one hundred years.*

One hundred years was traditionally deemed to be the natural span of life of a human being in the initial stages of history. In later times, only extraordinary persons could attain that longevity. But even enjoying a long life, says Zhang Boduan, does not afford release from impermanence.

6   *Retribution for your faults is about to come — now you can hardly fool yourself.*

Here again Zhang Boduan adopts a Buddhist notion, the "retribution" for wrongful conduct, which results in an inferior reincarnation.

7-8 *If you do not search for the Great Medicine, how can you ever come upon it? But coming upon it and not refining it, this is truly foolish and insane.*

As Wang Mu remarks, these two sentences refer to the necessities of looking for a master, and of devoting oneself to self-cultivation, respectively.

Poem 3

1   *If you study immortality,*
you should study celestial immortality:
only the Golden Elixir
is the highest principle.
3   *When the two things meet,*
emotions and nature join one another;
where the five agents are whole,
Dragon and Tiger coil.

5   *Rely in the first place on wu and ji*
that act as go-betweens,
then let husband and wife
join together and rejoice.
7   *Just wait until your work is achieved*
to have audience at the Northern Portal,
and in the radiance of a ninefold mist
you will ride a soaring phoenix.

其三

1   學仙須是學天仙
    惟有金丹最的端
3   二物會時情性合
    五行全處龍虎蟠

5   本因戊己為媒娉
    遂使夫妻鎮合歡
7   只候功成朝北闕
    九霞光裏駕翔鸞

NOTES ON POEM 3

In this poem, Zhang Boduan uses traditional images to describe the main features and benefits of the Golden Elixir. There are several grades of transcendence, but for the very fact of being graded, they pertain to the realm of relativity in which we live. Only "celestial immortality," says Zhang Boduan, grants complete transcendence, the removal of distinctions between the precelestial and postcelestial domains. Fulfilling the Way of the Golden Elixir is analogous to ascending to Heaven as an immortal and having audience with the highest deities.

1   *If you study immortality, you should study celestial immortality.*

The word translated as "immortality" (*xian*) means, more precisely, "transcendence." In the view of *Awakening to Reality*, celestial immortality is the highest degree of realization. Taoist texts contain several descriptions of the grades of transcendence. For example, the *Zhong Lü chuandao ji* (Records of the Transmission of the Dao from Zhongli Quan to Lü Dongbin), a work probably dating from the tenth century, states in the section entitled "On True Immortality": "Immortality is not of one kind only. . . . There are five degrees of Immortals, namely, the demon immortals (*guixian*), the human immortals (*renxian*), the earthly immortals (*dixian*), the spirit immortals (*shenxian*), and the celestial immortals (*tianxian*)."

3   *When the two things meet, emotions and nature join one another.*

The "two things" are, fundamentally, True Yin and True Yang. Inner nature (*xing*) is essentially pure and unaffected by phenomena or events of any kind. Emotions (*qing*, a word also translated as feelings, sentiments, or passions) are often impure and tend to disjoin from one's nature, to the point that they may become uncontrolled. According to many Neidan texts, the separation of inner nature and emotions is a feature of the conditioned state in which we live. Only when True Yin and True Yang merge can one's inner nature and emotions be not independent of one another, but in agreement with one another.

The Chinese view of "emotions" is more complex than it might at first seem. Emotions are not seen as merely psychological phenomena, but rather as pertaining to the sphere of existence, of one's being in the world as an individual entity. For this very reason, emotions are often at odds with one's inner nature, which is inherently transcendent. When emotions and inner nature join one another, emotions turn into qualities —personality, temperament, attitudes—that allow a person to express his or her inner nature in life, according to his or her individuality.

4   *Where the five agents are whole, Dragon and Tiger coil.*

The five agents are Wood, Fire, Soil, Metal, and Water (see tables 2 and 3). They represent the differentiation of the One into the many, and the diverse qualities taken on by Original Breath (*yuanqi*) in the conditioned state. Soil is an emblem of the original unity of the five agents. "The five agents are whole" refers to the reversal to unity, which is performed first by reducing the five agents to three, and then to one (see Poem 14). Therefore the undividedness of the five agents is analogous to the joining of Yin and Yang.

The Dragon stands for True Yin within Yang, also symbolized by the inner line of the trigram Li ☲, and the Tiger stands for True Yang within Yin, also symbolized by the inner line of Kan ☵. They are the "two things" mentioned in the previous line. Kan ☵ and Li ☲ are born from the union of Qian ☰ and Kun ☷, the True Yang and True Yin of the precelestial state. To generate the world, Qian entrusts its creative essence to Kun, and becomes Li; Kun receives the essence of Qian to bring it to fulfillment, and becomes Kan. In Neidan, Kan and Li newly join together ("coil") and return their essences to one another. Symbolically, this liberates True Yin and True Yang from their residences in the conditioned state, and reestablishes the original pair of trigrams, namely Qian and Kun.

5   *Rely in the first place on* wu *and* ji *that act as go-betweens.*

Wu and *ji* are the two celestial stems related to the agent Soil (see table 4). Soil, which is placed at the center, is an emblem of the One giving birth to multiplicity. To generate the "ten thousand things," the One first divides itself into the Two, or Yin and Yang. The stems *wu* and *ji* respectively represent the Yang and the Yin halves of Soil, or the One.

In the human being, Soil is associated with the intention (*yi*), the faculty of focusing the mind on a goal or an object. In Neidan, the True Intention (*zhenyi*) brings about the union of Yin and Yang. This is possible because intention, just like Soil, embraces both Yin and Yang, or *wu* and *ji*.

For this reason, *wu* and *ji* are often said in Neidan texts to be the "go-betweens" (*meiping*) that allow the conjunction of Yin and Yang.

6   *Then let husband and wife join together and rejoice.*

Husband and wife respectively stand for the Yang and Yin principles, which join to generate the Elixir.

7-8 *Just wait until your work is achieved to have audience at the Northern Portal, and in the radiance of a ninefold mist you will ride a soaring phoenix.*

The expression *gong cheng*, translated above as "your work is achieved," can also mean "your merit is complete." — The Northern Portal (*beique*) is the gate of Heaven, and an emblem of the Center: the symbolic center of Heaven is at due North.

The imagery of these lines is similar to the one found in this passage of the *Cantong qi* (Token for Joining the Three, chapter 8):

> With the Way completed and virtue fulfilled,
> withdraw, stay concealed, and wait for your time.
> The Great One will send forth his summons,
> and you move your abode to the Central Land.
> Your work concluded, you ascend on high
> to obtain the Register and receive the Chart.

The last line of the *Cantong qi* passage refers to receiving consecration as an Immortal.

Poem 4

1   *This is the method of wondrous Reality*
within Reality,
where I depend on myself, alone
and different from all others.

3   *I know for myself how to invert,*
starting from Li ☲ and Kan ☵ :
who else can comprehend the floating and the sinking,
and determine the host and the guest?

5   *If in the Golden Tripod you want to detain*
the Mercury within the Vermilion,
first from the Jade Pond send down
the Silver within the Water.

7   *The cycling of fire in the spiritual work*
before the light of dawn
will cause the whole wheel of the Moon to appear
in the Deep Pool.

其四

1   此法真中妙更真
都緣我獨異於人

3   自知顛倒由離坎
誰識浮沈定主賓

5   金鼎欲留朱裏汞
玉池先下水中銀

7   神功運火非終旦
現出深潭月一輪

NOTES ON POEM 4

The topic of this poem is the "inversion" that produces the Golden Elixir. While True Yin and True Yang are separate from one another in the postcelestial world, the alchemical process allows them to conjoin. When they join, True Yin and True Yang reconstitute the state of precelestial Unity.

1   *This is the method of wondrous Reality within Reality.*

This line might be more literally translated as "This method is a wondrous Reality within Reality." It makes allusion to a passage of the *Daode jing* (Book of the Way and its Virtue, chapter 1): "These two (namely, the Dao as the unconceivable Absolute and the Dao as the creator or "mother" of the world) come forth together but have different names; both are called a mystery. Mystery within the Mystery, gate to all wonders."

2   *Where I depend on myself, alone and different from all others.*

This sentence derives in part from the *Daode jing* (Book of the Way and its Virtue, chapter 20): "I am alone and different from all others, and value being fed by the mother." (The "mother" is the Dao as the creator of the world.)

3   *I know for myself how to invert, starting from Li ☲ and Kan ☵.*

In the precelestial, unconditioned state, Qian ☰ (Heaven) is above, and Kun ☷ (Earth) is below. In the postcelestial, conditioned state, their places are taken by Li ☲ (Fire) and by Kan ☵ (Water), respectively (see table 7). Li and Kan harbor the True Yin and True Yang essences of the precelestial state. However, just like fire and water do in nature, Li and Kan respectively move upward and downward, and in doing so, they carry with them the true principles that they hold. True Yin and True Yang, therefore, are constantly separate from one another and cannot conjoin. In Neidan, one inverts the respective positions of Li ☲ (Fire) and Kan ☵ (Water): Li is moved below, and Kan is moved above. In this way, the upward and downward movements of Li and Kan allow True Yin and True Yang to meet. Their joining gives birth to the Elixir.

4 *who else can comprehend the floating and the sinking, and determine the*
   host and the guest?

This line mentions two pairs of technical terms that are common in Neidan texts. Their meaning is comprehensible on the basis of the remarks made in the previous note. "Floating and sinking" (*fuchen*) refers to Li ☲ (Fire) moving upward, and to Kan ☵ (Water) moving downward. "Host and guest" (*zhubin*) refers to the respective positions of Li and Kan. In the conditioned state, Li is above, and thus is the host (it is in command); Kan is below, and thus is the guest (it is subordinate). When the positions of Kan and Li are inverted, they return to perform the roles that pertain to them.

5-6 *If in the Golden Tripod you want to detain the Mercury within the Vermilion,*
     first from the Jade Pond send down the Silver within the Water.

These lines describe the alchemical process using terms and symbols drawn from different contexts (a similar imagery is used in Poem 10, lines 3-4). Like many other passages of *Awakening to Reality*, their subject is the joining of True Yin and True Yang.

With regard to the True Yin principle, the Golden Tripod (*jinding*) corresponds to the trigram Li ☲; it is Yang holding True Yin, represented by the central broken line. The trigram Li is associated with the mineral cinnabar, one of whose Chinese names is "vermilion sand" (*zhusha*). Cinnabar holds mercury, which is True Yin. This is what Zhang Boduan calls "the Mercury within the Vermilion."

With regard to the True Yang principle, the Jade Pond (*yuchi*) corresponds to the trigram Kan ☵; it is Yin holding True Yang, represented by the central solid line. The trigram Kan is associated with the agent Water. Water stands for Yin containing True Yang, which is referred to here as "silver" (the agent Water has the black color as its emblem, and silver is of the opposite color, white). Therefore Zhang Boduan uses the expression "Silver within the Water."

This makes it possible to understand the meaning of these lines. As we have seen, in the conditioned state Li is positioned above, and Kan is positioned below; this causes the continuous separation of True Yin and True Yang. In the Neidan process, their positions are inverted. When Kan (the Jade Pond) is placed above, True Yang (Silver within Water) can be "sent down." When Li (the Golden Tripod) is placed below, True Yin (Mercury within the Vermilion) does move upward and is "detained."

7-8 *The cycling of fire in the spiritual work before the light of dawn will cause the whole wheel of the Moon to appear in the Deep Pool.*

The "cycling of fire" is the same as the "fire times" (*huohou*) mentioned in the next poem; see the note to Poem 5, lines 5-6. One complete cycle of heating symbolically lasts one day and one night. (According to Wang Mu, instead, the expression "before the light of dawn" means that the Elixir is compounded in a short time.)

When the heating is completed, the Elixir takes form in the lower Cinnabar Field (*dantian*), here called Deep Pool (*shentan*). Zhang Boduan compares the Elixir to the "whole wheel of the Moon." This is an allusion to the fact that the Elixir is equivalent to Pure Yang (*chunyang*), a common name in Taoism for the state prior to the division of the One into Yin and Yang. It might at first seem odd that this state is described with the image of the full Moon. When the Moon is full, however, it is thoroughly exposed to the rays of the Sun; the full Moon, therefore, is an image of the elimination of the impurities of the conditioned state, associated with the Yin principle, and of the return to Pure Yang.

Poem 5

1   *The Tiger leaps, the Dragon soars,*
wind and waves are rough;
in the correct position of the center
the Mysterious Pearl is born.
3   *A fruit grows on the branches*
and ripens at the end of season:
could the Infant in the womb
be different from this?

5   *Between south and north, the ancestral source*
causes the hexagrams to revolve;
from daybreak to dusk, the fire times
accord with the Celestial Axis.
7   *You should know the great concealment*
while you dwell in the market place:
what need is there of entering the mountains' depths
and keeping yourself in stillness and solitude?

其五

1   虎躍龍騰風浪麤
    中央正位產玄珠
3   果生枝上終期熟
    子在胞中豈有殊

5   南北宗源翻卦象
    晨昏火候合天樞
7   須知大隱居廛市
    何必深山守靜孤

NOTES ON POEM 5

This poem is concerned with the "fire times" (*huohou*). Fire (heat) is gradually increased and then decreased in several cyclical stages. The model for its circulation is provided by the ascent and descent of the particle of Primordial Yang in the cosmos, which in turn coincides with the apparent movement of the Northern Dipper at the center of heaven.

1-2 *The Tiger leaps, the Dragon soars, wind and waves are rough; in the correct position of the Center the Mysterious Pearl is born.*

The Tiger represents True Yang within Yin, and the Dragon represents True Yin within Yang. Having been liberated from their temporary residences in Kan ☵ and Li ☲, out of which they "leap" and "soar," Tiger and Dragon give rise to "wind and waves": the Tiger is traditionally associated with wind, and the Dragon, with rain (the "waves"). When Tiger and Dragon join in the Center, they give birth to the Elixir, the Mysterious Pearl (*xuanzhu*). With regard to the human being and the alchemical practice, the "correct position of the center" is the lower Cinnabar Field (*dantian*; see the note to Poem 7, line 5).

The term Mysterious Pearl derives from a tale in the *Zhuangzi* (chapter 12), where it denotes spiritual awareness or insight beyond intellectual knowledge, sense perceptions, and the discursive mind. "The Yellow Emperor went wandering north of the Red Water, ascended the slopes of Mount Kunlun, and gazed south. When he arrived at home, he discovered that he had lost his Mysterious Pearl. He sent Knowledge to look for it, but Knowledge couldn't find it. He sent the keen-eyed Li Zhu to look for it, but Li Zhu couldn't find it. He sent Wrangling Debate to look for it, but Wrangling Debate couldn't find it. At last he tried employing Shapeless, and Shapeless found it" (trans. Watson, *The Complete Works of Chuang Tzu*, 128-29, slightly modified).

3-4 *A fruit grows on the branches and ripens at the end of season: could the Infant in the womb be different from this?*

The process of conceiving, gestating, and giving birth to a child is one of the main images of the generation of the Elixir in Neidan. The symbolic "end of season" for the birth of the Infant is ten months after its conception: in China, gestation is traditionally deemed to last ten months.

5-6 *Between south and north, the ancestral source causes the hexagrams to revolve; from daybreak to dusk, the fire times accord with the Celestial Axis.*

As Zhang Boduan makes explicit, these lines refer to the "fire times" (*huo-hou*), the heating of the Elixir. The symbolism of Zhang Boduan's words is complex and is hardly comprehensible without reference to a parallel passage found in the *Cantong qi* (Token for Joining the Three, chapter 18):

> Moving in a ring in accordance with Jade-cog and Armil,
> rising and falling, ascending and descending,
> it flows in cycles through the six lines,
> and can be hardly beheld.
> Thus it has no constant position:
> it is the ancestor of change.

In this passage, the "ancestor of change" is True Yang, or the One Breath prior to Heaven (*xiantian yiqi*), which in the cosmos rises and declines following the directions of space and the cycles of time. Its continuous, circular movement through the time cycles is represented by the twelve "sovereign hexagrams" (*bigua*, see table 8), which graphically depict its ascent and descent along the six lines of each hexagram. This movement accords with the apparent rotation of the Northern Dipper at the center of Heaven.

Zhang Boduan uses a very similar imagery. The "ancestor of change" of the *Cantong qi* is his "ancestral source." The "movement in a ring" is expressed by his words, "between south and north." Just as the "ancestor of change" in the *Cantong qi* "flows in cycles through the six lines" of the hexagrams, so does Zhang Boduan's "ancestral source" cause "the hexagrams to revolve." Finally, the rotation of the hexagrams is determined by the Northern Dipper, which is referred to in the *Cantong qi* by its second and third stars, Jade-cog (*xuan*) and Armil (*ji*), and by Zhang Boduan as Celestial Axis (*tianshu*), which is the name of the first star of the Dipper and, by extension, denotes the whole constellation placed at the center of Heaven.

In alchemical practice, the heating of the Elixir according to the "fire times" is modeled on the cycle of the twelve hexagrams. Heat is repeatedly increased and then decreased, forming the two main stages known as "Yang fire" (or "Yang heat," *yanghuo*) and "Yin response" (*yinfu*). Each cycle symbolically reproduces the rise of the Yang principle from midnight to midday, and its decline from midday to midnight. Zhang Boduan refers to these stages with the words "from daybreak to dusk."

Fan, rendered in line 5 as "revolve," might also be translated as "overturn." Regardless of the translation, the significance of the sentence is that the sequence of twelve hexagrams is formed by two sets of six hexagrams, and each hexagram in one set is the reverse of one hexagram in the other set (Fu ䷗ and Gou ䷫, Lin ䷒ and Dun ䷠, and so forth; see again table 8).

7-8 *You should know the great concealment while you dwell in the market place: what need is there of entering the mountains' depths and keeping yourself in stillness and solitude?*

These final lines emphasize that Neidan does not require any special external setting, and is entirely an inner process.

Poem 6

1 *All people on their own have*
the Medicine of long life;
it is only for insanity and delusion
that they cast it away to no avail.
3 *When the Sweet Dew descends,*
Heaven and Earth join one another;
where the Yellow Sprout grows,
Kan ☵ *and Li* ☲ *conjoin.*

5 *A frog in a well would say*
that there are no dragon lairs,
and how could a quail on a fence know
that phoenix nests exist?
7 *When the Elixir ripens, spontaneously*
Gold fills the room:
what is the point of seeking herbs
and learning how to roast the reeds?

其六

1 人人自有長生藥
  自是愚迷枉擺拋
3 甘露降時天地合
  黃芽生處坎離交

5 井蛙應謂無龍窟
  籠鷃爭知有鳳巢
7 丹熟自然金滿屋
  何須尋草學燒茅

NOTES ON POEM 6

The Golden Elixir is fundamentally possessed by every human being; it is an image of one's innermost true nature, and of its realization in one's existence. Its immaterial ingredients are the basic constituents of life, and their conjunction is the most natural of all processes that constantly occur in individual and universal existence.

3-4 *When the Sweet Dew descends, Heaven and Earth join one another; where the Yellow Sprout grows, Kan* ☵ *and Li* ☲ *conjoin.*

The term "sweet dew" (*ganlu*) derives from a passage of the *Daode jing* (Book of the Way and its Virtue, chapter 32): when the world followed the Dao, "Heaven and Earth were joined to one another, causing sweet dew to descend." In agreement with these words, which refer to the joining of Heaven and Earth, internal alchemy uses Sweet Dew as a synonym of the Elixir.

Yellow Sprout is a common alchemical term that connotes both True Lead (True Yang) and the initial stage of the Elixir. The yellow color refers to the association of the Elixir with Soil, the agent that resides at the center and that is made of Yin and Yang joined together (see the note to Poem 3, line 5). Kan and Li represent Yin and Yang.

Both Sweet Dew and Yellow Sprout, therefore, connote the Elixir. However, just like dew comes down from heaven and partakes of the nature of water, so does Sweet Dew refers to the Yang component of the Elixir, namely, the True Lead generated from Water. A sprout, instead, grows upward from the earth and partakes of the nature of wood; Yellow Sprout refers to the Yin aspect of the Elixir, or True Mercury, whose related agent is Wood (see tables 2 and 3).

Note again the references to time ("when") and space ("where") in lines 3 and 4, respectively; compare Poem 3, lines 3-4.

5 *A frog in a well would say that there are no dragon lairs.*

This line and the next one make allusion to passages of the *Zhuangzi*. For the present line, compare *Zhuangzi*, chapter 17: "You can't discuss the ocean with a well frog—he's limited by the space he lives in. . . . Now you have come out beyond your banks and borders and have seen the great sea—so you realize your own pettiness. From now on it will be possible to talk to you about the Great Principle" (trans. Watson, *The Complete Works of Chuang Tzu*, 175-76). For the next line, see the next note.

6   *And how could a quail on a fence know that phoenix nests exist?*

Compare the story found at the beginning of the *Zhuangzi* (chapter 1), where a quail says: "I give a great leap and fly up, but I never get more than ten or twelve yards before I come down fluttering among the weeds and brambles. And that's the best kind of flying anyway!" Zhuangzi comments: "Therefore a man who has wisdom enough to fill one office effectively, good conduct enough to impress one community, virtue enough to please one ruler, or talent enough to be called into service in one state, has the same kind of self-pride as these little creatures" (trans. Watson, *The Complete Works of Chuang Tzu*, 31).

7   *When the Elixir ripens, spontaneously Gold fills the room.*

The "room" (*wu*, a word also meaning "house") mentioned in this line has been understood either as a locus within the body or as the whole person.

8   *What is the point of seeking herbs and learning how to roast the reeds?*

Taoist texts often include compounding and ingesting herbal drugs among the so-called "minor arts" (*xiaoshu*). The final line of this poem is addressed to those who devote themselves to these methods.

Poem 7

1   *You should know that the source of the stream,*
the place where the Medicine is born,
is just at the southwest —
that is its native village.
3   *When Lead meets the birth of gui,*
quickly you should collect it:
if Metal goes past the full moon,
it is not fit to be savored.

5   *Send it back to the earthenware crucible,*
seal it tightly,
then add the Flowing Pearl,
so that they are match for one another.
7   *For the Medicine to weigh one pound*
the Two Eights are needed;
regulate the fire times
relying on Yin and Yang.

其七

1   要知產藥川源處
只在西南是本鄉
3   鉛遇癸生須急採
金逢望遠不堪嘗

5   送歸土釜牢封閉
次入流珠廝配當
7   藥重一斤須二八
調停火候託陰陽

NOTES ON POEM 7

This poem concerns an essential aspect of internal alchemy: the collection of True Yang, which is the initial ingredient of the Elixir. As soon as one comes upon True Yang—which in fact is continuously regenerated within the postcelestial domain, even though it is hidden from it—one should store it safely and let it join with one's True Yin, the fundamentally pure consciousness that underlies the cognitive mind.

1-2 *You should know that the source of the stream, the place where the Medicine is born, is just at the southwest — that is its native village.*

The symbolism of the first half of this poem is complex. The Medicine is True Yang. In the postcelestial domain (the world in which we live), True Yang is contained within Yin, and is represented by the unbroken line within Kan ☵. This line is the One Breath that Kun ☷ receives from Qian ☰ as they unceasingly stay joined to one another. On the one hand, therefore, the One Breath is hidden from the world (being concealed within Kan ☵), but on the other hand, it is constantly regenerated by Kun ☷. Since Kun, in the postcelestial domain, is positioned at the southwest (see table 7) Zhang Boduan says that "the place where the Medicine is born is just at the southwest," and calls this the "native village" of True Yang.

3-4 *When Lead meets the birth of gui, quickly you should collect it: if Metal goes past the full moon, it is not fit to be savored.*

These lines essentially repeat the concepts presented in the first two lines. True Yang here is represented by Lead. *Gui* is one of the two celestial stems associated with Water (see table 4); it stands, in particular, for the postcelestial aspect of Water, i.e., Kan ☵. In other words, Zhang Boduan says that Lead, or True Yang, should be collected as soon as it is born within Kun ☷. In the cycle of the lunar month, Yang culminates on the fifteenth day and then declines; therefore the full moon illustrates the symbolic "time" by which the collection of True Yang should happen.

5-6 *Send it back to the earthenware crucible, seal it tightly, then add the Flowing Pearl, so that they are match for one another.*

The term "earthenware crucible" (*tufu*) derives from external alchemy. In internal alchemy, it denotes the lower Cinnabar Field (*dantian*). The word

43

tu, translated as "earthenware," is also the term for Soil, which among the five agents represents the center. This explains why, in line 2 of Poem 5, Zhang Boduan refers to the lower Cinnabar Field saying: "in the correct position of the Center the Mysterious Pearl is born."

The Flowing Pearl (*liuzhu*) is True Mercury, which generates the Elixir when it joins True Lead. This term is an abbreviation of Flowing Pearl of Great Yang (*taiyang liuzhu*), which denotes True Yin within Yang. See the note to Poem 12, lines 3-4.

7-8 *For the Medicine to weigh one pound the Two Eights are needed; regulate the fire times relying on Yin and Yang.*

The expression "two eights" has two meanings in Neidan. First, in the traditional Chinese weight system, one pound (*jin*) corresponds to sixteen ounces (*liang*). The symbolic "pound" of Elixir, therefore, is made of eight ounces of Lead and eight ounces of Mercury. The second meaning is more complex and is related to the "fire times" based on the lunar cycle. The waxing quarter of the Moon is represented by the trigram Dui ☱, and its waning quarter is represented by the trigram Gen ☶. The waxing quarter occurs at the middle of the first half of the month, eight days after the black Moon (novilune); the waning quarter occurs at the middle of the second half of the month, eight days after the full Moon (plenilune). Therefore the waxing (Yang) and waning (Yin) quarters of the Moon—which actually appear in the night sky as "halves" rather than "quarters"—are both represented by the number 8, and constitute the "two eights." Since line 7 mentions the weight of "one pound," and line 8 states that one should "regulate and adjust the fire times relying on Yin and Yang," both meanings of the expression "two eights" are relevant to the present poem.

Poem 8

1   *Desist from refining the Three Yellows*
and the Four Spirits:
if you seek the common medicines,
none of them is the real thing.
3   *When Yin and Yang are of one kind,*
they conjoin;
when the Two Eights match one another,
they merge.

5   *The Sun is red at the pool's bottom,*
and Yin wondrously is exhausted;
the Moon is white at the mountain's peak,
and the Medicine puts forth new sprouts.
7   *The people of our times should comprehend*
True Lead and Mercury:
they are not the common sand
and quicksilver.

其八

1   休鍊三黃及四神
    若尋眾藥便非真
3   陰陽得類俱交感
    二八相當自合親

5   潭底日紅陰怪盡
    山頭月白藥苗新
7   時人要識真鉛汞
    不是凡砂及水銀

NOTES ON POEM 8

This poem opens with a criticism of external alchemy. Its practices are rejected because they do not make the joining of True Yin and True Yang possible. When the ingredients of the Elixir are of "one kind" with regard to one another, and to the constitution of the human being, they spontaneously conjoin. The Elixir symbolizes the state prior to the subdivision of the One into the Two, which is defined in internal alchemy, and in Taoism as a whole, as the state of Pure Yang (*chunyang*).

1   *Desist from refining the Three Yellows and the Four Spirits.*

These terms pertain to external alchemy; Zhang Boduan enjoins his readers to refrain from its practice, which at his time was declining but was still widespread. The Three Yellows are realgar (*xionghuang*), orpiment (*cihuang*), and sulphur (*liuhuang*). Their Chinese names all include the word "yellow": "male yellow," "female yellow," and "flowing yellow," respectively. The Four Spirits are cinnabar (*dansha*), quicksilver (*shuiyin*), lead (*qian*), and saltpeter (or other solvents, *xiao*).

3   *When Yin and Yang are of one kind, they conjoin.*

The principle of belonging to the "same kind" or the "same category" (*tonglei*) has been known since early times in Chinese thought, and later became one of the foundations of internal alchemy. In the tradition of internal alchemy, this principle has two main senses, both of which are present here. First, the ingredients of the Elixir should be of the "same kind" as the human being. For this reason, several authors criticize external alchemy and its use of minerals and metals, which do not match the human constitution. Secondly, the ingredients of the Elixir should be of the "same category" as the primary constituents of Being as a whole, namely True Yin and True Yang.

One of the first references to the principle of belonging to the "same kind" is found in the later chapters of the *Zhuangzi* (chapter 31): "Creatures [or: things] of the same kind follow one another, and a voice will answer to the voice that is like itself. This has been the principle of Heaven since time began" (see trans. Watson, *The Complete Works of Chuang Tzu*, 346).

4   *When the Two Eights match one another, they merge.*

On the Two Eights see above the note to Poem 7, line 7.

5-6 *The Sun is red at the pool's bottom, and Yin wondrously is exhausted; the Moon is white at the mountain's peak, and the Medicine puts forth new sprouts.*

The "pool's bottom" is the lower Cinnabar Field; compare Poem 4, line 8, where Zhang Boduan uses the term Deep Pool (*shentan*). The "mountain's peak" is the upper Cinnabar Field, which is sometimes depicted as a range of mountain peaks. The red color of the Sun is an image of Pure Yang (*chunyang*), the state in which the impurities associated with the Yin principle are removed (see the note to Poem 4, lines 7-8). The same, once again, is for the white color of the Moon (see the same note).

    According to another interpretation, the red color stands for True Yang that emerges from Water (Yin) in the lower Cinnabar Field. When True Yang is moved to the upper Cinnabar Field, its emblem is the white color of the Moon.

8   *They are not the common sand and quicksilver.*

The "common sand" is cinnabar, whose Chinese name literally means "cinnabar sand" (*dansha*) or "vermilion sand" (*zhusha*). Refining mercury (quicksilver, Yin) from native cinnabar (Yang) and adding it repeatedly to sulphur (Yang) until the Yin components would be entirely discarded was the central method of external alchemy. In the Neidan way of seeing, this method does not make the conjunction of True Yin and True Yang possible: instead of using two initial ingredients that are of "one kind," it is based on a single ingredient, cinnabar, which on its own represents only the Yang principle.

Poem 9

1 *The Yin essence within Yang*
is not a firm substance:
if you cultivate only this thing
you will become ever more weak.
3 *Toiling your body by pressing and pulling*
is certainly not the Way,
ingesting breath and swallowing mist
is entirely foolish.

5 *The whole world recklessly tries*
to subdue Lead and Mercury —
when will they be able to see
Dragon and Tiger submitted?
7 *I exhort you to probe and grasp*
the place where one comes to life:
return to the fundament, revert to the origin,
and you are a Medicine King.

其九

1 陽裏陰精質不剛
獨修此物轉羸尪
3 勞形按引皆非道
服氣餐霞總是狂

5 舉世謾求鉛汞伏
何時得見龍虎降
7 勸君窮取生身處
返本還元是藥王

NOTES ON POEM 9

Like Poem 8, this poem also refers to erroneous practices: cultivating "the Yin essence within Yang" (instead of the Yang essence within Yin), performing *daoyin* and massage, and carrying out breathing exercises. These practices do not make it possible for True Yin and True Yang to join one another, which is equivalent to returning to "the place where one is generated."

1   *The Yin essence within Yang is not a firm substance.*

This line refers to the essence, or rather the essences, found within the body, some of which are at the center of the practices criticized in the present poem. Compare these verses of the *Zhixuan pian* (Pointing to the Mystery), a work attributed to Zhongli Quan:

> Tears, saliva, semen, juices, breath, blood, and liquids:
> These seven things are entirely Yin.

Chen Zhixu (1290-after 1335), who quotes the *Zhixuan pian* verses in his *Jindan dayao* (Great Essentials of the Golden Elixir, chapter 3), adds: "Only the Essence prior to Heaven and Earth belongs to Yang, and this is what the saints cultivate to make the Elixir."

3   *Toiling your body by pressing and pulling is certainly not the Way.*

Anyin ("pressing and pulling") is a shortened form of *anmo daoyin* ("pressing and rubbing" and "guiding and pulling"). *Daoyin* is a form of gymnastics based on postures that favor the circulation of breaths and essences found within the body. *Anmo* is usually rendered as "massage." *Daoyin* and *anmo*, however, are essentially identical. According to the definition found in the *Yiqie jing yinyi* (Pronunciations and Meanings of All the Scriptures, chapter 10), "When one practices rubbing and pushing by oneself, and extends and contracts one's own limbs as a means to remove toiling and eliminate vexations, this is called *daoyin*. If one does the same onto the body of another person, sometimes rubbing it and sometimes pushing it, it is called *anmo*."

4   *Ingesting breath and swallowing mist is entirely foolish.*

"Swallowing mist" is often mentioned together with "ingesting breath" (*fuqi*) and with "drinking dew" (*yinlu*). As remarked by Paul Crowe in his translation of *Awakening to Reality*, "this practice involves specifically inhaling the dawn mists. It is at this time that the red and yellow *qi* of the sun begins to emerge" ("*Chapters on Awakening to the Real*," 29, note 95). There is a poetical antecedent for the phrase "ingesting breath and swallowing mist" in a composition by Bai Juyi (772-846), one of the greatest Chinese poets:

> In the Abbey of the Jade Mushroom, the retired master Wang
> ingests breath and swallows mist to nourish himself skillfully.

5-6   *The whole world recklessly tries to subdue Lead and Mercury; when will they be able to see Dragon and Tiger submitted?*

"Making Lead and Mercury subdue" and "making the Dragon and the Tiger submit" both refer to allowing Yin and Yang to join one another. Neidan texts often refer to the coupling of Yin and Yang as "making the Dragon submit and the Tiger subdue" (*jianglong fuhu*) or as "making the Dragon and the Tiger submit and subdue" (*jiangfu longhu*). — The word *man*, translated above as "recklessly," has a wide range of other meanings, including "idly," "unendingly," and "everywhere."

7   *I exhort you to probe and grasp the place where one comes to life.*

According to one interpretation, "the place where one comes to life" is the lower Cinnabar Field (*dantian*), where the Elixir—often represent as an embryo—is generated. It is also possible to understand this sentence in a purely figurative sense, with reference to the ultimate source of existence; this is suggested, in fact, by the next line, which mentions "returning to the fundament" and "reverting to the origin."

8   *Return to the fundament, revert to the origin, and you are a Medicine King.*

In addition to being the appellation of a Buddha (or a Bodhisattva), Medicine King (*yaowang*) was a title given to eminent doctors. Here, however, the allusion is in the first place to the Elixir, which *Awakening to Reality* and many other alchemical texts often call "the Medicine" (*yao*). Wang Mu, who in this instance follows the commentary by Lu Xixing

(1520-1601 or 1606), suggests instead that the Elixir itself, and not the one who compounds it, is the "King of Medicines."

Poem 10

1   *Hold True Lead firmly*
and seek with intention;
do not let time
easily slip by.
3   *Just let the earthly po-soul*
seize the Mercury in the Vermilion,
and and you will have the celestial hun-soul by itself
controlling the Metal in the Water.

5   *One can say that when the Way is lofty,*
Dragon and Tiger are subdued,
and it may be said that when Virtue is hefty,
gods and demons are restrained.
7   *Once you know that your longevity*
equals that of Heaven and Earth,
troubles and vexations have no way
to rise to your heart.

其十

1 好把真鉛著意尋
莫教容易度光陰
3 但將地魄擒朱汞
自有天魂制水金

5 可謂道高龍虎伏
堪言德重鬼神欽
7 已知壽永齊天地
煩惱無由更上心

NOTES ON POEM 10

This poem is about True Yin and True Yang that control one another and join together to generate the Elixir. This process is regulated and actuated by the True Intention (*zhenyi*).

1   *Hold True Lead firmly and seek with intention.*

Intention (*yi*) is the principle that allows the alchemical process to occur. It is related to Soil, the central agent that represent the unity of Yin and Yang and makes their conjunction possible. (See the note to Poem 3, line 5.)

3-4   *Just let the earthly po-soul seize the Mercury in the Vermilion, and you will have the celestial hun-soul by itself controlling the Metal in the Water.*

The "earthly *po*-soul" is True Yang found within Yin; it is the precelestial Original Essence of which the physical body is a Yin manifestation. Analogously, the "celestial *hun*-soul" is True Yin found within Yang; it is the precelestial Original Spirit of which the thinking mind is a Yang manifestation.

The "Mercury in the Vermilion" is True Mercury, or True Yin within Yang. It is found within Fire, which is represented in alchemy by native cinnabar (called in Chinese *zhusha*, lit. "vermilion sand"). The "Metal in the Water" is True Lead, or True Yang within Yin. In the system of the five agents, Metal is found within Water. (Zhang Boduan uses a similar terminology in Poem 4, lines 5-6.)

In the postcelestial world, the Yang principle tends to rise to Heaven and vanish above, causing the loss of True Yin; the Yin principle tends to descend into the Earth and be wasted below, causing the loss of True Yang. To avoid this, the precelestial *po*-soul (True Yang) should control the Yin principle (the "Mercury in the Vermillion"), and the precelestial *hun*-soul (True Yin) should restrain the Yang principle (the "Metal in the Water").

7   *Once you know that your longevity equals that of Heaven and Earth.*

True longevity is immortality, or transcendence.

Poem 11

1   *The Yellow Sprout and the White Snow*
are not difficult to seek;
to attain them, you must rely
on deeply virtuous conduct.
3   *The four images and the five agents*
all avail themselves of Soil,
and as for the Three Origins and the eight trigrams,
could they be separate from ren?

5   *The refined numinous substance*
is difficult for us to comprehend:
it dispels all evil spirits,
and no demon will trespass.
7   *I am about to leave the secret instructions*
to all of you,
but have never heard of anyone
who appreciates them.

其十一

1   黃芽白雪不難尋
達者須憑德行深
3   四象五行全藉土
三元八卦豈離壬

5   鍊成靈質人難識
消盡群魔鬼莫侵
7   欲向人間留祕訣
未聞一箇是知音

NOTES ON POEM 11

Finding True Yin and True Yang and joining them with one another is not difficult, provided that one models one's operation on the operation of the Dao, and lets one's behavior and activity to be guided from the innermost center. Zhang Boduan is showing us his teaching about how to achieve this, but fears that those who read his words will not understand them.

1 *The Yellow Sprout and the White Snow are not difficult to seek.*

Yellow Sprout (*huangya*) denotes True Yang within Yin (i.e., True Lead), and White Snow (*baixue*) denotes True Yin within Yang (i.e., True Mercury). Both names derive from external alchemy. (On the Yellow Sprout see also the note to Poem 6, line 4.)

2 *To attain them, you must rely on deeply virtuous conduct.*

This is one of the most important points in *Awakening to Reality*, in internal alchemy, and beyond. "Virtuous conduct" (*dexing*) does not—or at least, does not only—refer to ethical or moral behavior. According to the *Daode jing* (Book of the Way and its Virtue), "virtue" is in the first place the way in which the Dao operates (a formulation not entirely satisfying, since the Dao is said to operate by "non-doing"). The virtue of the saint, or the sagely person, is said in turn to consist in modeling one's behavior on the operation of the Dao. See, for example, chapters 10 and 51 of the *Daode jing*, which describe the virtue of the saint and the virtue of the Dao, respectively, using the same words: "Generating but not owning, doing without being dependent, letting grow without managing: this is called Mysterious Virtue."

3 *The four images and the five agents all avail themselves of Soil.*

The expression "four images" (*sixiang*) in this sentence can be understood in two different but equivalent ways. In the first sense, the four images are the Vermilion Bird, the Dark Warrior, the White Tiger, and the Green Dragon. These are the emblems of the four "external" agents, namely Fire, Water, Metal, and Wood, respectively (see table 3). In the second sense, the four images are the four primary trigrams, namely Qian ☰, Kun ☷, Kan ☵, and Li ☲. In this order, the trigrams are associated with the above-mentioned agents.

The central agent Soil represents the Unity that gives origin to and underlies multiplicity. The other four agents and the four trigrams represent the state of multiplicity.

4   *And as for the Three Origins and the eight trigrams, could they be separate from* ren?

The term Three Origins (or Three Primes, *sanyuan*) defines several entities in the Taoist tradition. Here, most likely, it refers to Original Essence, Original Breath, and Original Spirit. ("Original" is equivalent to "precelestial.") — For the eight trigrams, see table 6.

The celestial stem *ren* is associated with the North and stands for the precelestial aspect of Water. It is this Water that gives birth to True Lead, which in turn is, ultimately, the Elixir. (See also the note to Poem 7, lines 3-4.)

The Center and the North are closely related to one another: the cosmic North, represented by the Pole Star or by the Northern Dipper, is the Center of Heaven. Water is, moreover, the first agent to be generated in the "cosmogonic sequence" of the five agents (Water - Wood - Fire - Soil - Metal).

5   *The refined numinous substance is difficult for us to comprehend.*

The "refined numinous substance" is the Elixir.

6   *It dispels all evil spirits, and no demon will trespass.*

Evil spirits and demons pertain to the Yin principle. This line, therefore, alludes in the first place to the fact that the Elixir consists of Pure Yang (*chunyang*) and eliminates the negativities that pertain to the postcelestial domain.

Poem 12

1　In plants and trees, Yin and Yang
　　are equal to one another;
　　let either be lacking,
　　and they do not bloom.
3　First the green leaves open,
　　for Yang is the first to sing,
　　then a red flower blossoms,
　　as Yin follows later.

5　This is the constant Dao
　　that everyone uses daily;
　　but returning to the True Origin —
　　does anyone know about this?
7　I announce to all of you
　　who study the Dao:
　　if you do not comprehend Yin and Yang,
　　do not fiddle around.

其十二

1　草木陰陽亦兩齊
　　若還缺一不芳菲
3　初開綠葉陽先唱
　　次發紅花陰後隨

5　常道即斯為日用
　　真源反覆有誰知
7　報言學道諸君子
　　不識陰陽莫強嗤

57

NOTES ON POEM 12

In nature, the Yang principle precedes the Yin principle, but both of them are necessary: Yang gives the initial impulse to life, Yin brings it to achievement. The same priority of Yang over Yin is seen in the treatment of the ingredients of the Golden Elixir, when True Lead is first refined from "black lead" and is then joined to True Yin refined from cinnabar; and in the "fire times," where a Yang phase of increasing heat is followed by a Yin phase of decreasing heat. At the same time, however, the alchemical process is based on the "inversion" of the natural processes, which makes it possible to revert to the original state, here called the True Origin. Both movements—the forward and the backward ones—are needed in order to fulfill the alchemical path.

3-4 *First the green leaves open, for Yang is the first to sing, then a red flower blossoms, as Yin follows later.*

The green color is an emblem of the initial stage of the True Yang principle. The red color is the symbolic color of the Elixir, which "blossoms" when the True Yin principle joins the True Yang principle.

In their language, these verses mirror a passage of the *Cantong qi* (Token for Joining the Three, chapter 24): "The Golden Flower is the first to sing . . . The Yang (i.e., the Flowing Pearl of Great Yang) next goes to join it." Golden Flower (*jinhua*) is a common synonym of True Lead, or True Yang within Yin. Flowing Pearl of Great Yang (*taiyang liuzhu*) is a common synonym of True Mercury, or True Yin within Yang.

5 *This is the constant Dao that everyone uses daily; but returning to the True Origin — does anyone know about this?*

The expression "constant Dao" derives from the opening sentences of the *Daode jing* (Book of the Way and its Virtue): "A *dao* that can be designated as a *dao* is not the constant Dao; a name that can be designated as a name is not the constant Name." Here, however, "constant Dao" refers specifically to the "forward movement" (*shun*, lit. "continuation") that allows life—both in a universal and in an individual sense—to be generated and to develop, but ultimately results in death.

"Returning to the Origin" refers instead to the backward movement (*ni*, "inversion") that occurs in the alchemical process. Here the stages that lead to the emergence of life—in both senses mentioned above—are traced in a reverse sequence. Compare Poem 9, lines 7-8: "I exhort you to probe and grasp the place where you come to life: return to the fundament, revert to the origin, and you are a Medicine King."

Poem 13

1   *If you do not comprehend that within the Mystery*
there is an inversion and then again an inversion,
how can you know the beautiful lotus bud
within the Fire?
3   *Take the White Tiger back home,*
and nourish it:
you will give birth to a bright pearl
as round as the Moon.

5   *Desist from guarding the furnace of the Medicine*
and from watching over the fire times:
just settle the breathing of the Spirit
and rely on the celestial spontaneity.
7   *When all of Yin is entirely dispelled,*
the Elixir ripens:
you leap out of the cage of the mundane,
and live ten thousand years.

其十三

1   不識玄中顛倒顛
   爭知火裏好栽蓮
3   牽將白虎歸家養
   產箇明珠似月圓

5   謾守藥爐看火候
   但安神息任天然
7   群陰消盡丹成熟
   跳出凡籠壽萬年

NOTES ON POEM 13

After the introduction given in the previous poem, Zhang Boduan provides more details on the subject of "inversion." As soon as True Yang is recognized and collected, it should be moved "above" and be "sent down" (see Poem 4, lines 5-6) to join one's True Yin, the pure and empty consciousness that underlies the thinking mind. "Inversion" does nothing but reestablish the original state of being. After this, nothing needs to be done, and one enters the state of non-doing. The Elixir coalesces spontaneously, and one returns to the True Origin.

1   *If you do not comprehend that within the Mystery there is an inversion and then again an inversion.*

This line might be translated more literally as: "If you do not understand how to invert the inversion within the Mystery." Internal alchemy is concerned with two "inversions." The first one occurs with the generation of the cosmos and the entrance in the postcelestial, conditioned state: in this state, True Yang is found within Yin, and True Yin is found within Yang. The second inversion occurs with the alchemical process, which releases the original principles from their postcelestial dwellings and restores the original state of being.

2   *How can you know the beautiful lotus bud within the Fire?*

In nature, the lotus plant grows in water. The "lotus bud" is taken therefore as an image of the inner line of Kan ☵ (Water). In the alchemical process, this line, which stands for True Yang, is returned to its place within Li ☲ (Fire).

3-4 *Take the White Tiger back home, and nourish it; you will give birth to a bright pearl as round as the Moon.*

The White Tiger is associated with the West and the trigram Kan ☵. Therefore these verses refer once again to moving the inner Yang line of this trigram and bringing it "back home" to the central position within Li ☲, in order to generate the Elixir (the "bright pearl").

5-6 *Desist from guarding the furnace of the Medicine and from watching over the fire times; just settle the breathing of the Spirit and rely on the celestial spontaneity.*

After the elixir has been generated, one needs to nourish it. Accordingly, the heating according to the cycle of the "fire times" (see the note to Poem 5, lines 5-6) is no longer needed; it is replaced by an extremely subtle form of breathing performed with Original Spirit (*yuanshen*).

The translation of *manshou* as "desist from guarding" differs from those found in other versions of *Awakening to Reality*, which include "staying relaxed," "gradually guard," and "longuement gardez." This translation is based on Liu Yiming's commentary and on Wang Mu's explications of these lines. Both Liu Yiming and Wang Mu refer to the fact that, at this stage, one gradually enters from the state of "doing" (*youwei*) to the state of "non-doing" (*wuwei*), which in the third and last stage will be crucial to ensure the birth of the Infant. Liu Yiming's commentary will be quoted later in the present book. As for Wang Mu, he writes: "At this time, the Elixir has already coalesced; one should nourish it warmly, and it is not necessary to perform again the 'fire times.' As the process has reached the stage of 'refining breath into spirit,' [Zhang Boduan] clarifies that there is no more need of 'doing'" (*Wuzhen pian qianjie*, 23, note 5).

7 *When all of Yin is entirely dispelled, the Elixir ripens.*

Once again, Zhang Boduan points out that the compounding the Internal Elixir eliminates all impurities associated with the Yin principle (see also above, Poem 4, lines 7-8, and Poem 8, lines 5-6).

8 *You leap out of the cage of the mundane, and live ten thousand years.*

The basic meaning of the word *fan*, translated above as "mundane," is "normal, ordinary."

Poem 14

1   *Three, Five, One —*
all is in these three words;
but truly rare are those who understand them
in past and present times.
3   *East is 3, South is 2,*
together they make 5;
North is 1, West is 4,
they are the same.

5   *Wu and ji dwell on their own,*
their birth number is 5;
when the three families see one another,
the Infant coalesces.
7   *The Infant is the One*
holding True Breath;
in ten months the embryo is complete —
this is the foundation for entering sainthood.

其十四

1   三五一都三箇字
古今明者實然稀
3   東三南二同成五
北一西方四共之

5   戊己身居生數五
三家相見結嬰兒
7   嬰兒是一含真氣
十月胎圓入聖基

NOTES ON POEM 14

This poem describes the compounding of the Internal Elixir in terms of the five agents; it provides an example of the inversion that was the subject of the previous poem. The inversion process here consists in joining Wood and Fire, on the one hand, and Metal and Water, on the other hand. When this is done, there are two ingredients, namely True Yin and True Yang. Through the mediation of Soil, the central agent that partakes of the nature of both, Yin and Yang merge and generate the Elixir.

1   *Three, Five, One — all is in these three words.*

The first part of this line might also be understood as meaning "The three fives are one." On the meaning of these numbers, see the following notes.

3-4 *East is 3, South is 2, together they make 5; North is 1, West is 4, they are the same.*

These lines are based on the "generative numbers" (*shengshu*, or precelestial numbers, lit. "birth numbers") associated with the five agents (see tables 2 and 3). The four external agents are reduced to two by reintegrating those that represent the postcelestial state into those that represent the precelestial state: Wood (East, 3) is reintegrated into Fire (South, 2); Metal (West, 4) is reintegrated into Water (North, 1). As shown below, each dyad has a numeric value of 5.

WOOD + FIRE	3+2 = 5	inner nature + Original Spirit
METAL + WATER	4+1 = 5	emotions + Original Essence

In this way, inner nature returns to partake of Original Spirit, and emotions are turned into qualities manifested in the world of form.

5-6 Wu *and* ji *dwell on their own, their birth number is 5; when the three families see one another, the Infant coalesces.*

Wu and *ji* are the two celestial stems associated with the central agent, Soil (see table 4, and the note to Poem 3, line 5). Soil represents Intention (*yi*, the driving force of the alchemical process), and its "birth number" (i.e., its "generative number," or precelestial emblematic number) is 5.

There are therefore three entities, which Zhang Boduan calls "the three families": True Yin, True Yang, and the Intention. Each has a numeric value of 5 (the "three fives") and is in a balanced relation to the others. When True Yin and True Yang join through the mediation of Soil (the Intention), even the distinction between them, and between Spirit and the world of form, comes to an end. In the words often found in Neidan texts, "Form and Spirit are both wondrous" (*xingshen ju miao*).

It should be added that although one is bound to describe this process as occurring in stages, it happens synchronously, in one instant. One can say, for example, that Metal returns to Water and Wood returns to Fire, and then True Yin and True Yang join one another. But one can also say, vice versa, that the return of Metal to Water and of Wood to Fire is the result of the joining True Yin and True Yang. The "process" and the "result," in other words, are not only temporally simultaneous, but are identical. This suggests that the emblematic configuration described by Zhang Boduan in this poem is, in fact, nothing but a way to explain a fundamental point—the return to the state of Unity—by means of cosmological and alchemical emblems.

7   *The Infant is the One holding True Breath.*

According to the emblematic configuration seen above, when Mercury and Lead, or True Yin and Yang, are joined to one another in the Elixir, the five agents have returned to the state of Unity. The Infant, or the Elixir, represents the state in which Yin and Yang are not separated from one another, which is often described as the time—or timelessness—before the creation of the cosmos. Therefore the Infant carries, and restores, the True Breath of the One, prior to its division into the Two and the "ten thousand things."

8   *In ten months the embryo is complete — this is the foundation for entering sainthood.*

The mention of "ten months"—as mentioned earlier, gestation is traditionally deemed to last ten months in China—shows that this poem, like the previous one, refers to the second stage of the practice, "refining breath into spirit" (*lianqi huashen*). This is the stage in which the Elixir, having being generated in a way analogous to the conception of an embryo, is nourished in the womb. — The expression *rushengji*, translated above as "[this is] the foundation for entering sainthood," could also be read *ru shengji*, or "[this is] entering the foundation of sagehood." The translation given above takes into account several other expressions that include the term *rushen*, such as *chaofan rushen*, or "transcending the ordinary and entering sainthood," a Chan Buddhist locution borrowed by several Neidan texts.

Poem 15

1 *If you do not comprehend that True Lead*
is the proper ancestor,
the ten thousand practices
will all be vain exercises:
3 *leaving your wife and staying in idle solitude*
will separate Yin and Yang,
and cutting off the grains will only cause
your stomach to be empty.

5 *Herbs and trees and gold and silver*
are all dregs,
clouds and mist and Sun and Moon
partake of haziness;
7 *and as for exhaling and inhaling,*
or visualizing and meditating,
these pursuits are not the same
as the Golden Elixir.

其十五

1 不識真鉛正祖宗
萬般作用枉施功
3 休妻謾遣陰陽隔
絕粒徒教腸胃空

5 草木金銀皆滓質
雲霞日月屬朦朧
7 更饒吐納并存想
總與金丹事不同

NOTES ON POEM 15

As he has done in several previous poems, Zhang Boduan here criticizes several approaches to self-cultivation, such as celibacy, abstention from cereals, ingestion of herbal and alchemical drugs, breathing techniques, and visualization of the inner deities. All these methods pertain to what Neidan texts often refer to as the "side gates" (the literal translation of *pangmen*), i.e., inadequate techniques of realization. In the perspective of *Awakening to Reality*, only the knowledge of True Lead, which gives birth to the Elixir and is ultimately equivalent to it, is effective to achieve true realization.

1-2 *If you do not comprehend that True Lead is the proper ancestor, the ten thousand practices will all be vain exercises.*

True Lead (Yang within Yin) is the "proper ancestor" because it is the basis for making the Internal Elixir.

3-4 *Leaving your wife and staying in idle solitude will separate Yin and Yang, and cutting off the grains will only cause your stomach to be empty.*

Line 3 refers to maintaining celibacy. In line 4, "cutting off the grains" (*jueli*) is equivalent to "abstaining from cereals" (*bigu*), the common name of one of the practices for Nourishing Life (*yangsheng*). Cereals were deemed to leave dregs in the intestines that feed the three corpses (*sanshi*) and the nine worms (*jiuchong*), the agents of death residing within the human body. Some practitioners, therefore, replaced cereals with other substances, including herbs, minerals, and most importantly breath (*qi*).

5-6 *Herbs and trees and gold and silver are all dregs, clouds and mist and Sun and Moon partake of haziness.*

Line 5 alludes to ingesting herbal medicines or alchemical elixirs. In line 6, Zhang Boduan criticizes the methods for absorbing external breath (*qi*) and those for ingesting the essences (*jing*) of the Sun and the Moon.

7-8 *And as for exhaling and inhaling, or visualizing and meditating, these pursuits are not the same as the Golden Elixir.*

"Exhaling and inhaling" refers to breathing practices. The term used by Zhang Boduan, *tuna*, is a common abbreviation for *tugu naxin*, lit. "exhaling the old and inhaling the new [breaths]." "Visualizing and meditating" (*cunxiang*) refers to methods based on the visualization of the inner gods.

Poem 16

1   *The scriptures of the Immortals, ten thousand scrolls,*
all tell one thing:
only the Golden Elixir
is the ancestor, the root.

3   *Relying on the other in the position of Kun* ☷,
it comes to life and acquires a body,
then it is planted within the house of Qian ☰,
in the Palace of Conjunction.

5   *Do not marvel that the mechanism of Heaven*
is now entirely disclosed:
it is only because students
are deluded and dull.

7   *If you are able to understand*
the central meaning of my poems,
you will behold at once the Most High Elders
of the Three Clarities.

其十六

1   萬卷仙經語總同
金丹只此是根宗
3   依他坤位生成體
種向乾家交感宮

5   莫怪天機都漏泄
卻緣學者自迷蒙
7   若人了得詩中意
立見三清太上翁

Translation

NOTES ON POEM 16

All alchemical texts are concerned with one subject: the conjunction of Yin and Yang. In the sixteen "regulated verses" of his *Awakening to Reality*, Zhang Boduan has revealed the entire doctrine of the Golden Elixir. Understanding the meaning of these poems grants access to the highest Heavens.

1   *The scriptures of the Immortals, ten thousand scrolls, all tell one thing.*

Compare this passage of the *Cantong qi* (Token for Joining the Three, chapter 13):

> The Records of Fire count six hundred chapters:
> their import is equal, and they do not delude.

(The "Records of Fire" are the texts in the Elixir. In several editions of the *Cantong qi*, the second sentence is even closer to Zhang Boduan's words: "their import is equal, and they do not differ.")

3-4 *Relying on the other in the position of Kun ☷, it comes to life and acquires a body, then it is planted within the house of Qian ☰, in the Palace of Conjunction.*

The "other" is True Yang, the seed of the Elixir, which in the postcelestial state lies hidden within Kun ☷ as the inner line of Kan ☵. In the postcelestial arrangement of the eight trigrams, the "position of Kun" is the southwest (see table 7, and compare Poem 7, lines 1-2: "You should know that the source of the stream, the place where the Medicine is born, is just at the southwest — that is its native village"). The Palace of Conjunction is Li ☲; it is said to be found within Qian ☰ because Qian becomes Li as it bestows its generative essence onto Kun. These verses mean, therefore, that True Yang should be liberated from the place it occupies in the postcelestial world, and be brought back into Li ☲ to restore Qian ☰.

With regard to the human being, the "position of Kun" and the "house of Qian" are the lower and the upper Cinnabar Fields, which are respectively located in the abdomen and the head. In the last stage of the alchemical practice, the Elixir that was generated in the lower Cinnabar Field and was nourished in the central Cinnabar field (in the region of the heart) is moved to the upper Cinnabar Field.

71

These lines of *Awakening to Reality* bear a clear trace of a passage found in the *Ruyao jing* (Mirror for Compounding the Medicine), an earlier seminal Neidan text:

> It is born in Kun
> and is planted in Qian;
> as long as you are thoroughly sincere,
> the conjunction happens spontaneously.

5-6 *Do not marvel that the mechanism of Heaven is now entirely disclosed: it is only because students are deluded and dull.*

"Mechanism of Heaven" (*tianji*) here refers to the secret revealed by the doctrines of the Golden Elixir. Like several other Neidan authors, Zhang Boduan says that he felt compelled to write his work in order to transmit those doctrines to students of the alchemical art who are victims of doubt and erroneous views. Compare again the *Cantong qi* (Token for Joining the Three, chapter 13):

> How could a lowly man like I dare to heedlessly write
> what the worthies debated alone?
> But if I tied my tongue and remained dumb,
> I would cause a break in the Way and would incur punishment.
> And yet, should I write all the facts on bamboo and silk,
> I would fear all the same to disclose the tally of Heaven.

The "tally of Heaven" (*tianfu*) of the *Cantong qi* is equivalent to Zhang Boduan's "mechanism of Heaven."

8 *you will behold at once the Most High Elders of the Three Clarities.*

The Three Clarities (Sanqing) are the three highest heavens in Taoist cosmography. Arranged hierarchically from the higher to the lower one, they are the Heavens of the Jade Clarity (Yuqing), of the Highest Clarity (Shangqing), and of the Great Clarity (Taiqing). In this order, they are also the residences of the supreme Taoist deities, which Zhang Boduan calls here the Most High Elders, namely Yuanshi tianzun (Celestial Worthy of Original Commencement), Lingbao tianzun (Celestial Worthy of the Numinous Treasure), and Daode tianzun (Celestial Worthy of the Way and Its Virtue). As his name indicates, the third deity is Laozi in his deified form; his function is to act as a bridge between the celestial and the human worlds.

As remarked by Wang Mu, the deities mentioned in this line are images of the highest state of spiritual realization. Thus the initial sentence of the "Regulated Verses" of *Awakening to Reality*, "If you do not search for the Great Dao and do not leave the delusive paths," finds a counterpart in the final sentence, "you will behold at once the Most High Elders of the Three Clarities."

Selections from

Liu Yiming's Commentary

[Commentary on Poem 3, line 2: "*Only the Golden Elixir is the highest principle.*"]

Human beings receive this Golden Elixir from Heaven. It is perfectly good with nothing bad in it, it is innate knowledge (*liangzhi*) and innate capacity (*liangneng*).[21] It is the Numinous Root, entirely achieved and with nothing lacking. It is the Breath of precelestial Perfect Yang. . . .

Golden Elixir is another name for one's inchoate fundamental nature (*xing*).[22] There is no other Golden Elixir outside one's fundamental nature. Every human being has this Golden Elixir complete in oneself: it is entirely achieved in everyone. It is neither more in a sage, nor less in an ordinary person. It is the seed of the Immortals and the Buddhas, the root of the worthies and the sages.

However, when it is not refined by fire, Yang culminates and necessarily becomes Yin, completion culminates and necessarily becomes lacking. One falls into the postcelestial state. . . . Therefore the sages of antiquity established the Way of the Return [to the original state] through the Golden Elixir, so that everyone could go back to one's home and recognize one's ancestor, and revert to what one fundamentally and originally has in oneself.

[Commentary on Poem 8, lines 5-6: "*The Sun is red at the pool's bottom, and Yin wondrously is exhausted; the Moon is white at the mountain's top, and the Medicine puts forth new sprouts.*"]

The numinous root of the one particle of innate knowledge and innate capacity fundamentally arises from within Empty Non-Being. It is similar to the red Sun which rises from the bottom of a pool, and on its own extinguishes Yin, and it seems like the supine moon suspended above the top of a mountain, which causes the herbs to put forth new sprouts.

[21] The terms "innate knowledge" and "innate capacity" derive from one of the main Confucian texts, the *Mengzi* (chapter 7): "What one is able to do without learning is called innate capacity; what one knows without pondering is called innate knowledge."

[22] By using the adjective "inchoate" (*hun*), Liu Yiming immediately suggests the affinity between one's original nature and the Dao. "There is something inchoate and yet accomplished, born before Heaven and Earth. . . . I do not know its name, but call it Dao" (*Daode jing*, chapter 25).

Essentially, when the correct Breath is generated, the evil breaths spontaneously retire; and when the real returns, the artificial is dispelled. The redness of the Sun at the pool's bottom and the whiteness of the Moon on the mountain's peak are both images of the emergence of True Yang and the reappearance of the celestial mind (*tianxin*).[23] With the reappearance of the celestial mind, both knowledge and capacity return to their innate state. This is called the Golden Elixir.

This Golden Elixir is the True Yin and True Yang that one fundamentally possesses of one's own. It is formed by the joining of the firm and the yielding. It is the real treasure of one's nature being accomplished, and of one's existence being perfected. Could this ever be achieved by roasting and refining common cinnabar and quicksilver?

PRECELESTIAL AND POSTCELESTIAL

[Commentary on Poem 3, lines 3-4: *"When the two things meet, emotions and nature join one another; where the five agents are whole, Dragon and Tiger coil."* This passage provides an example of how Liu Yiming explains the relation between the precelestial and the postcelestial states of being.]

The Way of Cultivating the Elixir (*xiudan*) is nothing more than harmonizing the firm and the yielding, making strength and compliance match one another, and making nature and emotions join one another. When nature and emotions join, *Yin and Yang meet* and *the five agents are whole*. This is the boundless norm of Heaven.

The five agents are the five breaths of Metal, Wood, Water, Fire and Soil. In the precelestial state, these five breaths are the five origins,[24] namely Original Nature, Original Emotions, Original Essence, Original Spirit, and Original Breath. In the postcelestial state they are the "five things" (*wuwu*), namely the wandering *hun*-soul, the ghostly *po*-soul, the Yin essences, the cognitive spirit (*shishen*), and the errant intention.[25]

---

[23] The term *tianxin* also denotes the symbolic "heart of Heaven," or center of the cosmos.

[24] I.e., the basic constituents of the human being in their original, uncorrupted state.

[25] On the *hun*-soul and the *po*-soul see above the note to Poem 10, lines 3-4. On the Yin essences see above the note to Poem 9, line 1. The "discriminating spirit" is the thinking mind. The "errant intention" is the common intention, different from the True Intention that makes the joining of Yin and Yang possible;

The five origins include the five virtues, which are benevolence, righteousness, propriety, wisdom, and sincerity.[26] The "five things" include the "five thieves" (*wuzei*), which are pleasure, anger, grief, joy, and lust. When *the five agents are whole*, the precelestial and postcelestial are gathered together, and the five origins control the "five things."

HUMAN MIND AND MIND OF THE DAO

[Commentary on Poem 4, lines 5-6: "*If in the Golden Tripod you want to detain the Mercury within the Vermilion, first from the Jade Pond send down the Silver within the Water.*"]

The human mind pertains to Li ☲ (Fire). Li ☲ is rooted in the body of Qian ☰ (Heaven), and is the Golden Tripod. Fire possessing Earth, whose number is 2, is conscious knowledge (*lingzhi*).[27] At its center there is something yielding and compliant that comes from the Palace of Kun ☷ (Earth): it is the fundamental innate capacity (*liangneng*).

The human mind is fundamentally empty and cavernous, a void consciousness without taste. As it meets with the postcelestial cognitive spirit (*shishen*), it employs consciousness to produce illusion: it looks at shadows and raises dust, it follows the wind and lifts up waves, without a moment of pause. It is like *the Mercury within the Vermilion*, which flies away when it meets fire: it is extremely difficult to detain it. This is what the *Cantong qi* means when it says: "The Flowing Pearl of Great Yang desires ever to leave you."[28]

The mind of the Dao pertains to Kan ☵ (Water). Kan ☵ is rooted in the body of Kun ☷ (Earth), and is the Jade Pond. Water storing Heaven, whose number is 1, is true knowledge (*zhenzhi*).[29] At its center there is something firm and strong that comes from the Palace of Qian ☰ (Heaven): it is the fundamental innate knowledge (*liangzhi*).

see above the note to Poem 3, line 5.

[26] These are the five so-called "Confucian" virtues.

[27] "Fire possessing Earth" refers to the trigram Li ☲. This trigram represents Fire (Yang), but its inner Yin line belongs to Kun ☷, the trigram that represents Earth. The symbolic number of Earth is 2.

[28] Liu Yiming quotes these words from the *Cantong qi*, chapter 24. The Flowing Pearl of Great Yang is Mercury; see the note to Poem 12, lines 3-4.

[29] "Water storing Heaven" refers to the trigram Kan ☵. This trigram represents Water (Yin), but its inner Yang line belongs to Qian ☰, the trigram that represents Heaven. The symbolic number of Heaven is 1.

Because of the fall into the postcelestial state, with its evil breaths and pursuits of activities, the correct Yang recedes, Yang is trapped within Yin, and the real is covered by the artificial. One sinks into the ocean of desires, and innate knowledge is obscured, like Silver in Water; it is exhausted and barely exists. Silver is one in kind with Metal; the Silver within Water is the Metal stored within Water. In the precelestial state, this Metal is the innate knowledge of one's fundamental nature; in the postcelestial state, is it the true knowledge of the mind of the Dao. Being true knowledge, it is extremely firm and extremely strong, and therefore metaphorically it is called True Lead. Being true knowledge, it achieves immortality and the Dao, and therefore metaphorically it is called True Seed (*zhenzhong*).

All the sages and the worthies of antiquity collected this one ingredient, the Great Medicine, in order to fulfill their nature and existence. Although the conscious knowledge of the human mind moves easily, it can be controlled if it finds the real knowledge of the mind of the Dao. Then consciousness reverts to reality, and does not fly away. This is what the *Cantong qi* means when it says: "When, at last, it finds the Golden Flower, it turns around, and each relies on the other."[30]

... If you want to detain the conscious knowledge of the human mind, you must first send down this true knowledge of the mind of the Dao. Underneath the True Seed of true knowledge is a host that is not affected by contaminated breaths. The conscious knowledge of the human mind spontaneously coalesces and does not disperse itself.

By employing the mind of the Dao to control the human mind, one complies with the mind of the Dao by means the human mind; one commands conscious knowledge by true knowledge; and one nourishes true knowledge by conscious knowledge. The firm and the yielding match one another,[31] strength and compliance are like one thing, and nature and emotions join one another in harmony. Within a mid hour,[32] they coalesce into a round luminous jewel, numinously bright and shining, and the Yin deviant breaths can no more make any harm.

---

[30] These words also come from the *Cantong qi*, chapter 24.

[31] The same sentence (*gangrou xiangdang*) is found in the *Cantong qi*, chapter 2.

[32] This expression is also used by other authors of Neidan texts. The "hour" meant here is the *zi* hour (symbolically placed around the midnight, and formally corresponding to 11 PM — 1 AM). The "mid hour" is the first half of the *zi* hour, in which True Yang is born within the darkness of Yin.

MALE TIGER AND FEMALE DRAGON

[Commentary on Poem 5, lines 1-4: *"The Tiger leaps, the Dragon soars, wind and waves are rough; in the correct position of the center the Mysterious Pearl is born. A fruit grows on the branches and ripens at the end of season: could the Infant in the womb be different from this?"*]

The Way of the Great Elixir is the work of one instant. This instant is joined in its virtue with Heaven and Earth, in its light with the Sun and Moon, in its pattern with the four seasons, and in its destiny with gods and spirits.[33] It is hard to find and easy to miss. If there is even the slightest negligence, the Breath of the True Unity prior to Heaven is obtained and then is lost again. The Breath of the True Unity prior to Heaven is the Reverted Elixir.[34] Since the Reverted Elixir is formed by joining the two breaths, the firm and the yielding, it is called Breath of the True Unity; it does not mean that there is a separate Breath of the True Unity outside the Reverted Elixir.[35]

When the Reverted Elixir is obtained, the mind of the Dao is firm and strong, and the human mind is yielding and compliant; true knowledge and conscious knowledge become one. Round and bright, it is the beginning of life. It is innate knowledge and innate capacity, silent and immovable, responding to external stimuli, something belonging to one's "original face."[36] As its nature is firm, it is called True Lead; as its breath is strong, it is called Male Tiger (*xionghu*). Both True Lead and the Male Tiger are a single overflowing breath,[37] perfectly good with nothing bad in it, which preserves the celestial reality (*tianzhen*) of innate knowledge and innate capacity.

---

[33] These sentences derive from the "Commentary on the Words of the Text" ("Wenyan zhuan") on the hexagram Qian ☰ in the *Book of Changes*.

[34] Reverted Elixir (*huandan*) is a classical name of the Elixir in both external and internal alchemy. It refers, essentially, to the fact that its material or immaterial ingredients have reverted to their original state.

[35] In other words, there is no difference whatsoever between the Elixir and the precelestial True Unity.

[36] "Original face" (*benlai mianmu*) is a popular Chan (Zen) expression that connotes one's original nature.

[37] This expression originally derives the *Mengzi* (chapter 2), where the author says: "I am skillful in nourishing my overflowing breath (*haoran zhi qi*)" Liu Yiming and other Taoist authors took this as a name of the One Breath prior to Heaven.

After you recover this celestial reality, you must return it to the time before your father and mother gave birth to you,[38] and to the place where the five agents to not reach.[39] Then you can acquire the everlasting and indestructible celestial reality. Therefore when you have recovered the celestial reality, keep it warm and nourish it, seal it carefully and store it safely. In utter void and deep stillness, the Yang Breath is complete; when within utter stillness there is again movement, the numinous sprout appears. This is the time that Ancestor Lü talked about when he said:

> In the eternal instant of midnight,
> keep the Lead tripod warm:
> its radiance will break through the curtains.[40]

At that time, the radiance of Yang emerges from its lair, as strong as a male tiger. Its might cannot be restrained. Quickly greet it with the particle of Fire of empty consciousness within your true nature. This Fire of empty consciousness is called Female Dragon (*pinlong*). *The Tiger leaps, the Dragon soars* is an image for Yin and Yang gathering together; *wind and waves are rough* means that wind is generated when the Tiger emerges from its lair, and waves are raised when the Dragon emerges from its pool: Yin and Yang contend with one another. When Dragon and Tiger meet, nature and emotions seize one another. They join and become one, entering the Center.

The Breath prior to Heaven comes from empty Non-being; it coalesces and becomes a round pearl. The Embryo of Sainthood (*shengtai*)[41] acquires an image. The Embryo of Sainthood is the Spirit of the Valley (*gushen*), which is the spirit of the Mysterious and the Female that have joined as one.[42] The Mysterious, which is Yang, is the Tiger, which is the

---

[38] *Fumu weisheng qian* is another well-known expression found in Chan Buddhist texts. It has also been understood as meaning "the time before your father and mother were born."

[39] This expression is found, either in this or in slightly variant forms, in several Neidan texts.

[40] These verses are quoted from the *Qinyuan chun* (Spring in the Garden by the Qin River), an alchemical poem attributed to Lü Dongbin.

[41] The translation of *shengtai* as Embryo of Sainthood is based on Liu Yiming's own explanation of this term in his *Xiangyan poyi* (Smashing Doubts on Metaphorical Language), where he defines *shengtai* as "the Embryo of a Saint" (*shengren zhi tai*).

[42] These terms derive from the *Daode jing* (chapter 6): "The Spirit of the Valley never dies: it is called the Mysterious-Female. The gate of the Mysterious-Female

emotions; the Female, which is Yin, is the Dragon, which is nature. When nature and emotions join as one, the Embryo of Sainthood coalesces. The Mysterious-Female is established and the Spirit of the Valley is born.

When you reach this territory, all doing is concluded and non-doing appears. It is not necessary to do anything; just listen to what is so by itself. Similar to the day in which a fruit grown on a branch finally ripens, this is the time in which the Child in the belly is finally born.

But although the coalescence of the Embryo of Sainthood requires non-doing, there is still work to be done in order to prevent dangers and to use foresight against perils. Do not ignore this.

JOINING YIN AND YANG

[Commentary on Poem 8, lines 3-4: "*When Yin and Yang are of one kind, they conjoin; when the Two Eights match one another, they merge.*"]

Being of the same kind means that Yang is of one kind with Yin, and Yin is of one kind with Yang. *When Yin and Yang are of one kind*, the firm and the yielding respond to one another; they are like a husband and a wife who, having been separated for a long time, finally meet and conjoin.

With regard to the "two eights," Yang within Yin is True Yang, or balanced firmness and strength; Yin within Yang is True Yin, or balanced yieldingness and compliance. When the firm and the yielding return together to being balanced, Yin and Yang match one another with no unevenness or inequality. They spontaneously join and are intimate with one another. The inchoate One Breath coalesces and does not scatter.

When Yin and Yang are of one kind and *the Two Eights match one another*, the state prior to Heaven emerges from within the state posterior to Heaven. The mind of the Dao is firm and strong, and the human mind is yielding and compliant: true knowledge and conscious knowledge are two, but are joined together.

is called the root of Heaven and Earth. Unceasing and continuous, its operation never wears out." The term "mysterious" (*xuan*) typically refers to Heaven. Liu Yiming's explanation makes clear that the expression Mysterious-Female should be intended as formed by two correlated nouns ("the mysterious *and* the female") instead of an adjective and a noun ("the mysterious female").

THE BIRTH OF TRUE YANG

[Commentary on Poem 7, lines 1-2: "*You should know that the source of the stream, the place where the Medicine is born, is just at the southwest — that is its native village.*"]

The southwest is direction of Kun ☷, the land in which Fu ䷗ is reborn after the last day of the month, and in which Yin culminates and generates Yang.[43] In the human being, it is the time of the initial movement after quiescence culminates. This movement is the time of the emergence of the Great Medicine.

However, this movement is not the movement of emotions and desires arising from external stimuli; and it is not the movement of thoughts and ideas arising from the internal mind. It is the movement of innate knowledge of the celestial mind, the movement of the true knowledge of the mind of the Dao.

This innate knowledge of the celestial mind, this true knowledge of the mind of the Dao, can make one transcend the ordinary and enter sainthood,[44] rise from death and return to life; therefore they are represented by the image of the Medicine. At the time in which quiescence culminates and the ten thousand conditions are at rest, the innate knowledge of the celestial mind and the true knowledge of the mind of the Dao have a particle of radiance that reveals their origin; therefore they are represented by the image of the birth of the Medicine. The innate knowledge of the celestial mind and the true knowledge of the mind of the Dao are the white within the black; their movement is generated from quiescence, just like the source of a stream; therefore they are represented by the image of the source of a stream where the Medicine is born.

QIAN ☰ AND KUN ☷, KAN ☵ AND LI ☲

[Commentary on Poem 16, lines 3-4: "*Relying on the other in the position of Kun ☷, it comes to life and acquires a body, then it is planted within the house of Qian ☰, in the Palace of Conjunction.*"]

---

[43] As shown by its graphical representation, the hexagram Fu (lit., "Return") stands for the rebirth of the Yang principle after the obscuration of Yin, represented in turn by Kun ䷁.

[44] On this expression see above the note Poem 14, line 8.

In the position of Kun ☷, *it comes to life and acquires a body* refers to the one Yang within Kan ☵. *Within the house of Qian* ☰, *in the Palace of Conjunction* refers to the one Yin within Li ☲. Kan is fundamentally the body of Kun, therefore it says *in the position of Kun*; Li is fundamentally the body of Qian, therefore it says *within the house of Qian*.

With Qian it is easy to know, with Kun it is easy to do. Qian is firm and strong, Kun is yielding and compliant. By being firm and strong, it is easy to know and to avoid difficulties; by being yielding and compliant, it is simple to do and to refrain from forcing. In human beings, knowing easily and doing simply correspond to the fundamental nature of original innate knowledge and innate capacity.

. . . [When the original state of being is lost,] Yang is trapped within Yin, and the celestial reality is obscured. It is like Qian ☰ joining Kun ☷; the one Yang within Qian enters the palace of Kun, Kun becomes filled and forms Kan ☵. [Analogously,] Yin steals the position of Yang, and knowledge and cognition gradually develop. It is like Kun ☷ joining Qian ☰; the one Yin within Kun enters the palace of Qian, Qian becomes empty and forms Li ☲.

The Way of Cultivating the Elixir consists in reverting to Yang from within Yin; of extracting the true knowledge of the mind of the Dao and using it to transmute the conscious knowledge of the mind of man. When conscious knowledge returns to reality, and when true knowledge returns to consciousness, the mind of the Dao is firm and strong, and the mind of man is yielding and compliant. Yin and Yang conjoin, and the firm and the yielding respond to one another; strength and compliance match each other, and reality and consciousness do not scatter.

Then one reverts to one's initial innate knowledge and capacity, and to one's "original face." This is called "taking from Kan ☵ in order to fill up Li ☲," and "relying on Kun ☷ in order to plant Qian ☰."

CYCLING FIRE

[Commentary on Poem 4, lines 7-8: "*The cycling of fire in the spiritual work before the light of dawn will cause the whole wheel of the Moon to appear in the Deep Pool.*"]

The *spiritual work* is the careful and solitary work of silently cycling the light of Spirit. Fire is the harmonious breath of true knowledge and conscious knowledge, of the firm and the yielding joined as one. *Cycling fire* means being cautious about the unseen and attentive to the unheard.

In cycling this true knowledge and conscious knowledge, in joining the firm and the yielding as one, you should not leave a single grain of sediment in the "space of one square inch."[45]

The fire of the *spiritual work* is like setting up a pole and seeing its shadow, like shouting in a valley and transmitting the sound.[46] If you do this readily, *before the end of the day* you will be able to return to Yang from within Yin, like *the Sun appearing in a deep pool*[47] after the Yin breaths have retired.

THE "TWO SOILS" AND THE AUDIENCE AT THE NORTHERN PORTAL

[Commentary on Poem 3, lines 5-6: "*Rely in the first place on* wu *and* ji *that act as go-betweens, then let husband and wife join together and rejoice.*"]

After the original fundament of the precelestial state is lost and scattered, nature goes east and emotions go west,[48] and the firm and the yielding do not respond to one another. If there is no harmonizing thing that goes back and forth and mediates,[49] "that" and "this" separate and do not know one another.[50] What harmonizes is the two Soils, namely *wu* and *ji*.[51] The *wu*-Soil rules on movement and pertains to Yang. The *ji*-Soil rules on quiescence, and pertains to Yin. . . .

---

[45] This expression (*fangcun zhi jian*) denotes the lower Cinnabar Field in several Taoist texts.

[46] These images derive from the *Cantong qi* (chapter 2). They refer to "non-doing" as the unintentional but unfailing response to external or internal events and phenomena.

[47] Liu Yiming's text of *Awakening to Reality* has "the whole wheel of the Sun" instead of "the whole wheel of the Moon." See the note to Poem 4, lines 7-8.

[48] These words should be understood in a quite "literal" sense. See table 3, which shows that nature corresponds to the agent Wood (east), and emotions to the agent Metal (west).

[49] The term translated as "mediate," *tongxin*, literally means "to transmit a message," and refers to the function of Soil in bringing Yin and Yang to join one another (see the note to Poem 3, line 5). At the same time, *xin* also means "sincerity," the virtue associated with Soil mentioned by Liu Yiming in the next paragraph.

[50] "This" (*ci*) and "that" (*bi*, lit. the "other") are conventional terms in Neidan for the postcelestial and the precelestial, the "ten thousand things" and the Dao, the relative and the absolute, and other analogous pairs of notions or entities.

[51] See the note to Poem 3, line 5.

Within the five virtues, the two Soils, *wu* and *ji*, are true sincerity. When true sincerity is in the center, one's nature is stable. When true stability functions on the outside, one's emotions are harmonized. When nature is stable and emotions are harmonized, nature and emotions go back to the root: *husband and wife join together and rejoice.*

[Commentary on Poem 3, lines 7-8: "*Just wait until your work is achieved to have audience at the Northern Portal, and in the radiance of a ninefold mist you will ride a soaring phoenix.*"]

When benevolence, righteousness, propriety, and wisdom go back to the oneness of sincerity, and when nature, emotions, essence, and spirit meet in the One Breath, "the three families see one another,"[52] and "the five breaths have audience at the Origin."[53] You return to the origin and revert to the fundament, and the Golden Elixir coalesces; some call it the Embryo of Sainthood.

Continue to advance in your practice, passing from "doing" into "non-doing." Nourish [the Embryo] warmly for ten months, keeping it tightly closed [within the womb].[54] Lessen the excess of strong emotions, and augment the insufficiency of compliant nature.[55] Using the celestial True Fire, and relying on the hexagrams Zhun ䷂ in the morning and Meng ䷃ at night, smelt away the postcelestial Yin breaths.[56] Generate the immaterial from the material, passing from the subtle to the apparent. When the Breath is complete and Spirit is whole, "with a peal of thunder

[52] These words are quoted from Poem 14, line 6.

[53] This expression is found in many Neidan texts.

[54] Note the emphasis given on "closing," also found in texts of external alchemy where it applies, in a literal sense, to hermetically sealing the crucible.

[55] "Lessen" (*chou*) and "augment" (*tian*) are two other technical terms used in many Neidan texts. At this stage of the practice, Lead should be "lessened" and Mercury should be "augmented."

[56] This sentence refers to one of the ways in which the "fire times" are represented in internal alchemy. Sixty of the sixty-four hexagrams are associated with the thirty days of the lunar month. One pair of hexagrams, therefore, rules on each day; the first hexagram rules on its first half, and the second one, on its second half. Zhun and Meng are the first two hexagrams used in this cosmological pattern.

the golden cicada sheds its shell,"[57] and you have a body outside your body.

When the work is completed and your name is recorded,[58] you will *have audience at the Northern Portal* and will *ride a soaring phoenix.* You will fly and rise in the broad daylight,[59] and will become a Celestial Immortal of Pure Yang, free from death. Wouldn't that be pleasant?

CELESTIAL IMMORTALITY

[Commentary on Poem 3, line 1: "*If you study immortality, you should study celestial immortality.*"]

Those who fulfill both their nature and their existence, who have a body outside their body, whose form and spirit are both wondrous,[60] who are joined in their reality with the Dao, are celestial immortals.... Only the celestial immortals shed their illusory body and achieve a *dharmākaya* (*fashen*, the body of Buddhahood), go beyond creation and transformation,[61] and are without birth and without death. Being able to shed life and death, their longevity equals that of Heaven, and they last eternally without decaying.

---

[57] This is another expression found in many Taoist texts. It alludes to achieving an "immortal self," which Liu Yiming refers to at the end of the present sentence by saying, "you have a body outside your body."

[58] That is, one's name is entered in the "registers of immortality," according to the classical Taoist image for the achievement of transcendence.

[59] This sentence, which is frequent in Taoist texts, alludes to attaining the highest state of transcendence.

[60] As remarked above, this expression—which authors of Neidan texts use often—refers to the state of non-duality between formlessness and form, the Dao and the world, the absolute and the relative.

[61] I.e., they go beyond the manifested cosmos, which is ruled by change and impermanence.

Textual Notes

On the authors and the sources cited in this section see the "Note on the Translation" on p. 18. The variants reported below are found in the editions that I have consulted. In certain cases, they may be due to intentional or unintentional changes found only in those editions.

POEM 1

6. *Without considering that your body covertly withers and decays.* For "without considering" (*bugu* 不顧), Weng Baoguang (*Zhushu*) and Qiu Zhaoao have "without realizing" (*bujue* 不覺).

8. *Bribing impermanence would be impossible, wouldn't it?* For the translation of *bulai* 不來 as "impossible" see *Dai Kanwa jiten* 大漢和辭典, s.v. *bu* 不 (entry no. 19.1019, meaning no. 2). — The last word in this sentence, *wu* 無, is an interrogative particle similar to *fou* 否.

POEM 2

3. *Yesterday you were on the street riding on horseback.* For *fang* 方, the *Xiuzhen shishu*, Weng Baoguang (*Zhushi*), Lu Xixing, and Liu Yiming have *you* 猶: "Yesterday you were still on the street riding on horseback." — This line reads differently in Qiu Zhaoao's text: "Yesterday in your yard you were feasting and rejoicing" (昨日庭前方宴樂).

4. *This morning in your coffin you are already a sleeping corpse.* This line reads differently in Qiu Zhaoao's text: "This morning in your room you are sorrowful and grieved" (今朝室內已傷悲).

5. *Your wife and wealth are cast off, they are not in your possession.* For "cast off" (*pao* 拋) the *Xiuzhen shishu* has "left behind" (*yi* 遺).

7. *If you do not search for the Great Medicine, how can you ever come upon it?* For *zheng* 爭, Liu Yiming has *zhen* 真: "... can you truly come upon it?"

POEM 3

1. *If you study immortality, you should study celestial immortality.* Chen Zhixu's text has *sui* 雖 ("although") instead of *xu* 須 ("must, should"). I follow the reading found in all other sources that I have seen.

7. *Just wait until your work is achieved to have audience at the Northern Portal.* For "Northern Portal" (*beiguan* 北闕), the *Zhushu* version of Weng Baoguang's text has "Imperial Portal" (*diguan* 帝闕); the *Zhushi* version of Weng Baoguang's text and Lu Xixing have "Jade Portal" (*yuguan* 玉闕).

8. *And in the radiance of a ninefold mist you will ride a soaring phoenix.* For "soaring phoenix" (*xiangluan* 翔鸞), the *Xiuzhen shishu* and Weng Baoguang (*Zhushi*) have "auspicious phoenix" (*xiangluan* 祥鸞).

POEM 4

5. *If in the Golden Tripod you want to detain the Mercury within the Vermilion.* Chen Zhixu's text has *ruo liu* 若留 instead of *yu liu* 欲留. Although this variant has virtually no consequence on meaning, I follow the reading found in all other sources that I have seen.

7. *The cycling of fire in the spiritual work before the light of dawn.* For "before the light of dawn" (*fei zhongdan* 非終旦), the *Xiuzhen shishu* has "before the end of the night" (*fei zhongxi* 非終夕).

8. *Will cause the whole wheel of the Moon to appear in the Deep Pool.* For "the whole wheel of the Moon" (月一輪), the *Xiuzhen shishu*, Weng Baoguang (*Zhushu* and *Zhushi*), Lu Xixing, and Liu Yiming have "the whole wheel of the Sun" (日一輪). This reading eliminates any ambiguity on the meaning of this sentence.

POEM 5

4. *Could the Infant in the womb be different from this?* For "womb" (*bao* 胞), Liu Yiming has "belly" (*fu* 腹).

8. *What need is there of entering the mountains' depths and keeping yourself in stillness and solitude?* For *he bi* 何必 ("what need is there of . . . ?"), Chen Zhixu's text has *he bu* 何不 ("why not . . . ?"), which is certainly a textual error. I follow the reading found in all other sources that I have seen.

POEM 6

1. *All people on their own have the Medicine of long life.* For "of their own" (*zi* 自), the *Xiuzhen shishu* has "entirely" (*jin* 盡); Lu Xixing, Liu Yiming and Qiu Zhaoao have "fundamentally" (*ben* 本).

2. *It is only for insanity and delusion that they cast it away to no avail.* For *yumi* 愚迷, Lu Xixing, Liu Yiming, and Qiu Zhaoao have *mitu* 迷徒: "It is only those who follow delusive paths that throw it away to no avail."

POEM 7

3. *When Lead meets the birth of* gui, *quickly you should collect it.* For "meet," Weng Baoguang (*Zhushu* and *Zhishi*) has "see" (*jian* 見).

POEM 8

1. *Desist from refining the Three Yellows and the Four Spirits.* For "desist from refining" (*xiulian* 休鍊), Liu Yiming has "cultivating and refining" (*xiulian* 修鍊). His commentary, however, includes a quotation of this sentence that reads "desist from refining."

2. *If you seek the common medicines, none of them is the real thing.* For "common medicines" (*zhongyao* 眾藥), Weng Baoguang (*Zhushu*), Lu Xixing, Liu Yiming, and Qiu Zhaoao have "common herbs" (*zhongcao* 眾草); the *Zhishi* version of Weng Baoguang's text has "herbs and plants" (*caomu* 草木).

3. *When Yin and Yang are of one kind, they conjoin.* For "conjoin" (*ju jiaogan* 俱交感), the *Xiuzhen shishu*, Weng Baoguang (*Zhushi*), Liu Yiming, and Qiu Zhaoao have "return to being conjoined" (*gui jiaogan* 歸交感).

5. *The Sun is red at the pool's bottom, and Yin wondrously is exhausted.* For "exhausted" (*jin* 盡), all other sources that I have seen have "extinguished" (*mie* 滅).

POEM 9

1. *The Yin essence within Yang is not a firm substance.* This line reads differently in the *Xiuzhen shishu*: "Do not take hold of the solitary Yin in order to have Yang" (莫把孤陰為有陽; trans. Crowe, 29).

2. *If you cultivate only this thing you will become ever more weak.* For "this thing" (*ci wu* 此物), all other sources that I have seen have "one thing" (*yiwu* 一物).

4. *Ingesting breath and swallowing mist is entirely foolish.* For "ingesting breath" (*fuqi* 服氣), the *Xiuzhen shishu* and Weng Baoguang (*Zhushi*) have "refining breath" (*lianqi* 鍊氣). For the same term, Liu Yiming has "ingesting" (*fushi* 服食), but a quotation of this sentence in his commentary has "ingesting breath."

5. *The whole world recklessly tries to subdue Lead and Mercury.* For *jushi* 舉世, the *Xiuzhen shishu* and Qiu Zhaoao have *bishi* 畢世: "for the whole of their lives they recklessly try to subdue Lead and Mercury."

POEM 10

2. *Do not let time easily slip by.* Jiao 教 in this sentence is used in the sense of *shi* 使 or *ling* 令, "to cause" (*Hanyu dacidian* 漢語大詞典, s.v. *jiāo* 教, meaning no. 2).

POEM 11

6. *It dispels all evil spirits, and no demon will trespass.* For "all evil spirits" (*qunmo* 群魔), the *Xiuzhen shishu* and Weng Baoguang (*Zhushu* and *Zhushi*) have "the Yin evil spirits" (*yinmo* 陰魔); Lu Xixing, Liu Yiming, and Qiu Zhaoao have "the Yin *hun*-soul" (*yinhun* 陰魂).

8. *But have never heard of anyone who appreciates them.* For "have never heard" (*wei wen* 未聞), Weng Baoguang (*Zhushu* and *Zhushi*), Lu Xixing, Liu Yiming, and Qiu Zhaoao have "have never met" (*wei da* 未達).

POEM 12

6. *But returning to the True Origin — does anyone know about this?* For *fanfu* 反復, Weng Baoguang (*Zhushu*), Lu Xixing, Liu Yiming, and Qiu Zhaoao have *fan ci* 返此: "But the True Origin inverts it (*i.e., it inverts the "constant Dao"*) — does anyone know this?" The *Zhushi* version of Weng Baoguang's text has *fanben* 返本: "But the True Origin and the reversion to the fundament — does anyone know these?"

8. *If you do not comprehend Yin and Yang, do not fiddle around.* For "fiddle around" (*qiangchi* 強嗤), Weng Baoguang (*Zhushu*), Lu Xixing, Liu Yiming, and Qiu Zhaoao have "act at random" (*luanwei* 亂為).

POEM 13

6. *Just settle the breathing of the Spirit and rely on the celestial spontaneity.* For "just settle" (*dan an* 但安), the *Xiuzhen shishu* has "just observe" (*dan kan* 但看).

7. *When all of Yin is entirely dispelled, the Elixir ripens.* For "entirely dispelled" (*xiaojin* 消盡), all other sources that I have seen have "entirely removed" (*bojin* 剝盡).

8. *You leap out of the cage of the mundane, and live ten thousand years.* For "cage of the mundane" (*fanlong* 凡籠, lit. "cage of the ordinary"), Weng Baoguang (*Zhushu*), Lu Xixing, and Qiu Zhaoao have "cage" (*fanlong* 樊籠).

POEM 14

7. *The Infant is the One holding True Breath.* For *ying'er shi yi* 嬰兒是一, Weng Baoguang (*Zhushu*) has *shi zhi taiyi* 是知太一: "Therefore we know that the Great One holds True Breath."

POEM 15

4. *And cutting off the grains will only cause your stomach to be empty.* On the word *jiao* 教 see above the textual note to Poem 10, line 2. — Chen Zhixu's text has *cong* 從 (lit. "from," or "to follow") instead of *du* 徒 ("only"). I follow the reading found in all other sources that I have seen.

POEM 16

3-4. *Relying on the other in the position of Kun* ☷, *it comes to life and acquires a body, then it is planted within the house of Qian* ☰, *in the Palace of Conjunction.* In these sentences, *wei* 位 (lit. "position") and *xiang* 向 (lit. "direction") are virtually synonyms. See *Hanyu dacidian* 漢語大詞典, s.v. *xiang* 向, meaning no. 9, where this word is glossed both as *fangxiang* 方向 ("direction") and as *fangwei* 方位 ("position"). Weng Baoguang (*Zhushu* and *Zhushi*) replaces *xiang* 向 with *zai* 在 ("in, at"); this reading eliminates any ambiguity.

Glossary of Chinese Characters

anmo daoyin 按摩導引 ("pressing and rubbing" and "guiding and
   pulling")

anyin 按引 ("pressing and pulling")

Bai Juyi 白居易 (772-846)

Bai Yuchan 白玉蟾 (1194-1229?)

baixue 白雪 (White Snow)

beique 北闕 (Northern Portal)

Beizong 北宗 (Northern Lineage)

benlai mianmu 本來面目 ("original face")

bi 彼 ("that," "the other")

bigu 辟穀 (abstaining from cereals)

bigua 辟卦 (sovereign hexagrams)

bulai 不來 ("impossible")

chaofan rushen 超凡入聖 ("transcending the ordinary and entering
   sainthood")

Chen Nan 陳楠 (?-1213)

Chen Zhixu 陳致虛 (1290-after 1335)

chou 抽 ("to lessen")

chunyang 純陽 (Pure Yang)

ci 詞 (lyrics)

ci 此 ("this")

cihuang 雌黃 ("male yellow," orpiment)

Cuixu pian 翠虛篇 (The Emerald Emptiness)

cunxiang 存想 (visualizing and meditating)

Dai Qizong 戴起宗 (fl. 1332-37)

dansha 丹砂 (cinnabar)

dantian 丹田 (Cinnabar Field)

Daode jing 道德經 (Book of the Way and its Virtue)

Daoshu shier zhong 道書十二種 (Twelve Books on the Dao)

Daozang 道藏 (Taoist Canon)

Daozang jinghua 道藏精華 (Essential Splendors of the Taoist Canon)

dexing 德行 (virtuous conduct)

dixian 地仙 (earthly immortals)

dizhi 地支 (earthly branches)

fan 凡 ("mundane, normal, ordinary")

fan 翻 ("revolve, overturn")

fandao 反道 (returning to the Dao)

fangcun zhi jian 方寸之間 ("space of one square inch")

Fanghu waishi 方壺外史 (The External Secretary of Mount Fanghu)

fashen 法身 (the body of Buddhahood)

Fu 復 ("Return," name of hexagram)

fuchen 浮沈 ("floating and sinking")

fumu weisheng qian 父母未生前 ("the time before your father and mother
    gave birth to you," or "the time before your father and mother were
    born")

fuqi 服氣 (ingesting breath)

gangrou xiangdang 剛柔相當 ("the firm and the yielding match one
    another")

ganlu 甘露 (Sweet Dew)

gong cheng 功成 ("your work is achieved," "your merit is complete")

guixian 鬼仙 (demon immortals)

gushen 谷神 (Spirit of the Valley)

haoran zhi qi 浩然之氣 ("overflowing breath")

houtian 後天 (postcelestial or posterior to Heaven, lit. "after Heaven")

huandan 還丹 (Reverted Elixir)

Huandan fuming pian 還丹復命篇 (Returning to Life through the Reverted
    Elixir)

huangya 黃芽 (Yellow Sprout)

Huanyuan pian 還源篇 (Reverting to the Source)

hun 混 ("inchoate")

huohou 火候 (fire times)

ji 己 (one of the celestial stems)

ji 璣 (Armil, one of the stars of the Northern Dipper)

jiangfu longhu 降伏龍虎 ("making the Dragon and the Tiger submit and
    subdue")

jianglong fuhu 降龍伏虎 ("making the Dragon submit and the Tiger
    subdue")

jin 斤 (pound, a weight measure)

jin 金 (metal; gold)

Jindan dayao 金丹大要 (Great Essentials of the Golden Elixir)

Jindan sibai zi 金丹四百字 (Four Hundred Words on the Golden Elixir)

jinding 金鼎 (Golden Tripod)

jinhua 金華 (Golden Flower)

jiuchong 九蟲 (nine worms)

jueju 絕句 ("cut-off lines")

jueli 絕粒 ("cutting off the grains")

leifa 雷法 (Thunder Rites)

Li Daochun 李道純 (fl. 1288-92)

liang 兩 (ounce, a weight measure)

liangneng 良能 (innate capacity)

liangzhi 良知 (innate knowledge)

lianjing huaqi 鍊精化氣 (Refining Essence into Breath)

lianqi huashen 鍊氣化神 (Refining Breath into Spirit)

lianshen huanxu 鍊神還虛 (Refining Spirit and reverting to Emptiness)

lingzhi 靈知 (conscious knowledge)

Liu Haichan 劉海蟾 (fourth or fifth Quanzhen patriarch)

Liu Yiming 劉一明 (1734-1821)

liudao 六道 (six ways of conditioned existence)

liuhuang 硫黃 ("flowing yellow," sulphur)

liuqu 六趣 (six directions of reincarnation)

liuzhu 流珠 (Flowing Pearl)

Lu Xixing 陸西星 (1520-1601 or 1606)

Lü Dongbin 呂洞賓 (third or fourth Quanzhen patriarch)

lüshi 律詩 ("regulated verses")

man 謾 ("recklessly," "idly," "unendingly," "everywhere")

manshou 謾守 ("desist from guarding")

meiping 媒娉 ("go-between")

mitu 迷途 (delusive paths)

neidan 內丹 (internal alchemy)

ni 逆 (backward movement, "inversion")

pangmen 旁門 ("side gates")

qian 鉛 (lead)

Qigong yangsheng congshu 氣功養生叢書 (Collectanea on Qigong and Nourishing Life)

qing 情 ([1] emotions, feelings, sentiments, passions; [2] qualities)

Qinyuan chun 沁園春 (Spring in the Garden by the Qin River)

Qiu Zhaoao 仇兆鰲 (1638-1713)

Quanzhen 全真 (Complete Reality)

ren 壬 (one of the celestial stems)

renxian 人仙 (human immortals)

rusheng ji 入聖基 ("the foundation for entering sainthood")

Ruyao jing 入藥境 (Mirror for Compounding the Medicine)

sanjie 三界 (Three Realms)

sanshi 三尸 (three corpses)

sanyuan 三元 (Three Origins, Three Primes)

shen wai zhi shen 身外之身 ("a body outside one's body," "a self outside one's self")

shen 神 (Spirit)

shengren zhi tai 聖人之胎 ("the Embryo of a Saint")

shengshu 生數 ("generative numbers" or precelestial numbers, lit. "birth numbers")

shengtai 聖胎 (Embryo of Sainthood)

shentan 深潭 (Deep Pool)

shenxian 神仙 (spirit immortals)

Shi Tai 石泰 (?-1158)

shishen 識神 (cognitive spirit)

shuiyin 水銀 (quicksilver)

shun 順 (forward movement, lit. "continuation")

sixiang 四象 (four images)

taiji 太極 (Great Ultimate)

taiyang liuzhu 太陽流珠 (Flowing Pearl of Great Yang)

tian 添 ("to augment")

tianfu 天符 ("tally of Heaven")

tiangan 天干 (celestial stems)

tianji 天機 ("mechanism of Heaven")

tianshu 天樞 (Celestial Axis, one of the stars of the Northern Dipper)

Tiantai 天臺 (district in present-day Zhejiang)

tianxian 天仙 (celestial immortals)

tianxin 天心 ("celestial mind"; "heart of Heaven")

tianzhen 天真 ("celestial reality")

tonglei 同類 ("same kind" or "same category")

tongxin 通信 ("to mediate")

tu 土 (Soil)

tufu 土釜 ("earthenware crucible")

tugu naxin 吐古納新 ("exhaling the old and inhaling the new [breaths]")

tuna 吐納 ("exhaling and inhaling")

waidan 外丹 (external alchemy)

Weng Baoguang 翁葆光 (fl. 1173)

"Wenyan zhuan" 文言傳 ("Commentary on the Words of the Text")

wu 屋 (room, house)

wu 悟 (awakening)

wu 無 (interrogative particle, in Poem 1, line 8)

wuchang 無常 (impermanent, "non-constant")

wuwei 無為 (non-doing)

wuwu 五物 ("five things")

wuxing 五行 (five agents, five phases)

wuzei 五賊 ("five thieves")

Wuzhen pian 悟真篇 (Awakening to Reality)

Wuzhen pian jizhu 悟真篇集註 (Collected Commentaries to *Awakening to Reality*)

Wuzhen pian shiyi 悟真篇拾遺 (Supplement to *Awakening to Reality*)

Wuzhen pian xiaoxu 悟真篇小序 (A Short Introduction to *Awakening to Reality*)

Wuzhen pian zhushi 悟真篇註釋 (Commentary and Exegesis to *Awakening to Reality*)

Wuzhen zhizhi 悟真直指 (Straightforward Directions on *Awakening to Reality*)

wuzu 五祖 (five patriarchs)

xian tiandi sheng 先天地生 ("born before Heaven and Earth")

xian 仙 (immortal, immortality; transcendent, transcendence)

xiancai 賢材 ("worthiness and talent")

Xiangyan poyi 象言破疑 (Smashing Doubts on Metaphorical Language)

xiantian yiqi 先天一氣 (One Breath prior to Heaven)

xiantian 先天 (precelestial or prior to Heaven, lit. "before Heaven")

xiao 硝 (saltpeter)

xiaoshu 小術 (minor arts)

"Xici" 繫辭 ("Appended Sayings" [to the *Book of Changes*])

xin 信 (sincerity)

xing 性 (inner nature)

xingshen ju miao 形神俱妙 ("Form and Spirit are both wondrous")

xionghu 雄虎 (Male Tiger)

xionghuang 雄黃 ("male yellow," realgar)

xiudan 修丹 ("cultivating the Elixir")

Xiuzhen shishu 修真十書 (Ten Books for the Cultivation of Reality)

xuan 玄 ("mysterious")

xuan 璇 (Jade-cog, one of the stars of the Northern Dipper)

xuanzhu 玄珠 (Mysterious Pearl)

Xue Daoguang 薛道光 (1078?-1191)

Yang 陽

yanghuo 陽火 ("Yang fire" or "Yang heat")

yangsheng 養生 (Nourishing Life)

yao 藥 (Medicine)

yaowang 藥王 (Medicine King)

yi 一 (One, Unity)

yi 意 (intention)

Yijing 易經 (Book of Changes)

Yin 陰

yinfu 陰符 ("Yin response")

yinlu 飲露 ("drinking dew")

yiqi 一氣 (One Breath)

Yiqie jing yinyi 一切經音義 (Pronunciations and Meanings of All the Scriptures)

youwei 有為 ("doing")

yuanqi 元氣 (Original Breath)

yuanshen 元神 (Original Spirit)

yuchi 玉池 (Jade Pond)

Yuqing jinsi Qinghua biwen jinbao neilian danjue 玉清金笥青華祕文金寶內鍊丹訣 (Alchemical Instructions on the Inner Refinement of the Golden Treasure, a Secret Text from the Golden Casket of the Jade Clarity Transmitted by the Immortal of Green Florescence)

Zhang Boduan 張伯端 (author of the *Wuzhen pian*)

zhangfu 丈夫 ("great man")

zhen 真 (reality, truth, perfection)

zhenren 真人 (True Man)

zhenyi 真意 (True Intention)

zhenzhi 真知 (true knowledge)

zhenzhong 真種 (True Seed)

Zhixuan pian 指玄篇 (Pointing to the Mystery)

Zhongli Quan 鍾離權 (second or third Quanzhen patriarch)

Zhong Lü chuandao ji 鍾呂傳道記 (Records of the Transmission of the Dao from Zhongli Quan to Lü Dongbin)

Zhuangzi 莊子 (Book of Master Zhuang)

zhubin 主賓 ("host and guest")

zhusha 朱砂 (vermilion cinnabar)

zi 子 (the symbolic time of rebirth of the Yang principle)

Ziyang zhenren 紫陽真人 (True Man of Purple Yang)

Ziyang zhenren Wuzhen pian sanzhu 紫陽真人悟真篇三註 (Three Commentaries to *Awakening to Reality* by the True Man of Purple Yang)

Ziyang zhenren Wuzhen pian zhushu 紫陽真人悟真篇註疏 (Commentary and Subcommentary to *Awakening to Reality* by the True Man of Purple Yang)

Works Quoted

Baldrian-Hussein, "Zhang Boduan." In Fabrizio Pregadio, ed., *The Encyclopedia of Taoism*, 2:1220-22. London and New York: Routledge, 2008.

Bertschinger, Richard. *The Secret of Everlasting Life: The First Translation of the Ancient Chinese Text of Immortality*. Shaftesbury, Dorset: Element, 1994.

Boltz, Judith M. *A Survey of Taoist Literature: Tenth to Seventeenth Centuries*. Berkeley: Institute of East Asian Studies, University of California, 1987.

Cleary, Thomas. *The Inner Teachings of Taoism*. Boston and London: Shambhala, 1986.

Cleary, Thomas. *Understanding Reality: A Taoist Alchemical Classic*. Honolulu: University of Hawaii Press, 1987.

Crowe, Paul. "*Chapters on Awakening to the Real*: A Song Dynasty Classic of Inner Alchemy Attributed to Zhang Boduan (ca. 983-1081)." *British Columbia Asian Review* 12 (2000): 1-40.

Davis, Tenney L., and Chao Yün-ts'ung. "Chang Po-tuan of T'ien-t'ai, his *Wu Chên P'ien*, Essay on the Understanding of the Truth: A Contribution to the Study of Chinese Alchemy." *Proceedings of the American Academy of Arts and Sciences* 73 (1939): 97–117.

Davis, Tenney L., and Chao Yün-ts'ung. "Four Hundred Word Chin Tan of Chang Po-tuan." *Proceedings of the American Academy of Arts and Sciences* 73 (1939): 371–76.

Liu Guoliang 劉國樑 and Lian Yao 連遙. *Xinyi Wuzhen pian* 新譯悟真篇 [A new explanation of *Awakening to Reality*]. Taipei: Sanmin shuju, 2005.

Pregadio, Fabrizio, and Lowell Skar. "Inner Alchemy (Neidan)." In Livia Kohn, ed., *Daoism Handbook*, 464-97. Leiden: E. J. Brill, 2000.

Pregadio, Fabrizio, ed., *The Encyclopedia of Taoism*. London and New York: Routledge, 2008.

Robinet, Isabelle. *Introduction à l'alchimie intérieure taoïste: De l'unité et de la multiplicité. Avec une traduction commentée des Versets de l'éveil à la Vérité*. Paris: Éditions du Cerf, 1995.

Robinet, Isabelle. "Original Contributions of Neidan to Taoism and Chinese Thought." In Livia Kohn, ed., *Taoist Meditation and Longevity*

Techniques, 297-330. Ann Arbor: Center for Chinese Studies, University of Michigan, 1989.

Wang Mu 王沐. *Wuzhen pian qianjie (wai san zhong)*「悟真篇」淺解（外三種）[A simple explanation of *Awakening to Reality* and three other works]. Beijing: Zhonghua shuju, 1990.

Watson, Burton. *The Complete Works of Chuang Tzu*. New York: Columbia University Press, 1968.

Wilhelm, Richard. *The I Ching or Book of Changes*. Translated by Cary F. Baynes. New York: Bollingen, 1950.

Zhang Zhenguo 张振国. *Wuzhen pian daodu*「悟真篇」导读 [A guided reading of *Awakening to Reality*]. Beijing: Zongjiao wenhua chubanshe, 2001.

Golden Elixir Press
www.goldenelixir.com

Chinese Alchemy: An Annotated Bibliography of Works in Western Languages, by Fabrizio Pregadio (2009). 50 pp.

This bibliography contains about 300 titles of books and articles, with short annotations on their contents. It was first published in the journal *Monumenta Serica* in 1996. In addition to minor changes, the present version contains a final section listing books and articles published between 1995 and early 2009.

Index of Zhonghua Daozang (中華道藏書目總錄), by Fabrizio Pregadio (2009). viii + 108 pp. ISBN 9780984308200.

This index is divided into two parts. Part 1 contains a list of texts in the *Zhonghua Daozang* (Taoist Canon of China). Part 2 contains lists of texts used as "base editions" in the *Zhonghua Daozang*. The index also serves as a tool to easily locate texts of the *Zhengtong Daozang* (Taoist Canon of the Zhengtong Reign-Period) in the *Zhonghua Daozang*.

CPSIA information can be obtained
at www.ICGtesting.com
Printed in the USA
LVOW11s0745200417
531517LV00001B/100/P